good sex

starsignsstarsigns

good sex

starsignsstarsigns

Michele Knight

MQP
MQ Publications Ltd

Published by **MQ Publications Limited**
12 The Ivories, 6–8 Northampton Street
London N1 2HY
Tel: 020 7359 2244   Fax: 020 7359 1616
email: mail@mqpublications.com

TEXT © **Michele Knight** 2002
DESIGN: **Balley Design**

ISBN: 1-84072-405-6

3 5 7 9 0 8 6 4 2

Printed and bound in China

Introduction   7

ARies   8
tAURUS   26
gemini   44
CANCER   60
leo   76
VIRgo   94
libRA   110
SCORpio   126
SAgittARius   142
CApricorn   158
AquARius   174
pisces   192

About the Author   208
Picture Credits   208

Introduction

Did you ever want to know what a particular person would be like in bed? Is it true that all Scorpios are good in bed, as well as being cheaters? Are Virgos cold and virginal? *Star Signs, Good Sex* is here to answer all your questions.

Can you tell what someone is like as a lover just by knowing his or her star sign? Can just knowing about a star sign reveal that? Yes, it can! Your star sign is the planet of your ego and what you strive to be—including your sexuality.

Each star sign has a unique view on love and sex and here I reveal the good, the bad, and the miraculous of each sign. What are your lover's secret sexual fantasies? What can you do to drive your mate crazy beneath the sheets? The following astrological secrets should give you the tools to capture the passion of your lover and leave him or her begging for more.

Star signs have different strengths and weaknesses: Some are great at massage and romance, while others think foreplay is the name of a new computer game. Check out your own sexual secrets and decide where you can improve your sexual knowledge and skills to become the perfect lover!

ARies

March 21 – April 20

Star profile

ELEMENT	Fire
KEY WORDS	Dynamic, instinctual, extroverted, passionate, intense, spontaneous
ATTRACTED TO	Good looks, strength, vulnerability, princesses or princes, sexiness, adoration
RULER	Mars

Aries, you are passionate and beautiful, embodying an amazing array of qualities as a lover. When you love you love totally, but can't stand someone who is a pushover. You attract people who worship you, but in your heart you prefer a bit of a challenge and love the thrill of the chase. You consider yourself equal if not superior to all others, particularly sexually, and often can be found participating in dangerous sports side by side with your partner. Your ideal love match is someone who is strong, confident, and adventurous and who can handle your overwhelmingly huge love. You need lots of attention and affection from your partner but will more than double it in return. You will not tolerate being controlled.

In a relationship you like the freedom to go out with your friends. You rebel from jealousy and need someone who trusts you, then you will never let them down. You dislike routine and appreciate someone who is willing to take a risk. You are either totally committed, worshiping your partner, or you seek the constant thrill of the chase and avoid commitment. There is rarely any middle ground in your relationships.

The Mythology of Aries

Mars is your ruling planet. In Roman mythology Mars is the god of war and your challenge is to transform yourself into the god, or goddess, of love.

Mars was quick-tempered and capable of acting quickly. In love, Mars can be used to inspire you to act rapidly to capture your loved one. However, once the relationship is established, you need to learn to quell your warlike nature.

What we give out creates a ripple effect within our lives. Scorpio is similarly ruled by Mars, yet has a quieter approach to life. Remember that love is delicate and does not respond to demands.

Mars, god of war, ruler of Aries

MYTHOLOGY: Athena, the goddess of Aries

Athena is the goddess of Aries. You are like the intelligent Athena and have a warrior's heart. Athena is also the Greek goddess of wisdom, and unlike Mars she is the goddess of Battle rather than war. Although known as a virgin goddess, Athena herself decided to remain single and independent. She is a great deity to meditate with if love goes wrong, because she brings you back to your power. Arians hate breakups more than any other sign (for at least twenty-four hours) and feel like the world has ended. To receive Athena's help, just rub olive oil onto a candle during the waxing moon, light it, and ask Athena to heal your broken heart. Within days you should be back to your bouncy, Arian self.

The Importance of Trust

Building upon the hero/heroine myth and being the best you can be (not only for yourself but for your relationship as well) will bring you great rewards. You are fundamentally honest in a relationship and will not say that you are committed unless you truly are. You hate to lie, but can be seduced when your ego is pandered to. The most important thing to you in a relationship is that your loved one believes in you. If you have this, you know you can move mountains and change the world!

If your partner does not believe in you, you will be very tempted to live up to their negative expectations and be a philanderer of the highest order. If they lose faith in you, this will also kill your love and passion for your loved one. You give all of your heart, but faith is an important exchange. If you are trusted, you can forgive anything and will not let your partner down.

Love tends to come easily to you. Your disarming charm leads to many admirers and a huge number of friends. When you are really crazy about someone you tend to go charging in with seduction in your eyes and fire in your heart. To really focus your power and invoke the love you deserve, take the time to center yourself for a moment. You have nothing to prove and you are truly wonderful just the way you are. Chill out and back off. You're irresistible!

The *ARIAN* MAN

Arian men exude strength, and when you want to you can be a true knight in shining armor. There isn't much you wouldn't do to rescue a damsel in distress. You like very classical and feminine women, but also admire successful, creative types as long as they are womanly. Your ideal partner is someone who lets you take the lead and admires your strength, but is strong enough to keep you in check if you go too far off the rails.

FAMOUS ARIAN MEN
Warren Beatty • Napoleon Bonaparte • Marlon Brando • Charlie Chaplin • Harry Houdini

The *ARIAN WOMAN*

As an Arian woman you have a host of celebrity divas, listed below, to inspire you. You may notice that some of these charismatic and powerful women have not fared that well in love. They often prefer independence and a fabulous career.

In love you are an enigma. On one hand, you seek Mr. Right to sweep you off your feet; on the other, you want to be the boss.

FAMOUS ARIAN WOMEN
Bette Davis • Aretha Franklin • Sarah Michelle Gellar • Chaka Khan • Lucy Lawless • Sarah Jessica Parker • Diana Ross

Independent Aries lady Bette Davis and James Cagney embrace in Jimmy the Gent

Slow and Steady Wins the Race

Giving away all your feelings and wearing your heart on your sleeve— as admirable as it is—can lead to you resenting your partner's apparent secrecy. Most relationships disclose things one stage at a time, so reveal yourself chapter by chapter rather than giving the whole book away on the first date.

Practice being more like Scorpios, who are also a star sign ruled by Mars. Show flashes of that huge love inside, but also let your new partner work to unveil the many mysteries of your heart. Ironically, although some people misconstrue you and think you are an egomaniac, you actually don't have a big ego at all: just a childlike need to bring pleasure to others in addition to getting your own needs met. You're a show-off and a clown, but in a very innocent way. Most people find this delightful. Those who don't are probably just jealous of your apparent confidence. It is a strange and fascinating dichotomy: You find it hard to believe that you are loved and worshiped, even though you demand it! This is because you just see yourself as you!

You can shoot your mouth off and often expect it all to be forgotten in an instant. Your favorite way to make up is to have rampant, passionate sex. Sometimes your partners feel differently, and you take this as rejection! You can't help it: You feel that it is your duty to speak everything that you think and are quick to anger. Be a little more sensitive to others and you will get all you desire with your Aries charm.

You will wow your partner with over-the-top generosity and your intense passion. The more someone pulls back, the more you will pursue them, so if someone wants to truly capture the

sex tip • sex tip •

Before or during a love encounter, run a warm bath and sprinkle in red rose petals and a few drops of rose oil. This blends your passionate red energy with the gentle caress of love, soothing you and taking you into the sensual realms of your fiery passion.

attentions of your boisterous, cloven love gods and goddesses, he or she must play it cool. An Aries lover is the same in love as in all things: "I want it and I want it now." Instant gratification is the key word and you will act spontaneiously to sweep your lover off their feet. Sexually you can be too eager, and you sometimes want to get to the final act without the necessary foreplay.

Aries is the first sign in the Zodiac. You are instigators and leaders in all things, especially love. You charge in and are usually instinctual and impulsive in your choices. You need to be careful, however, as this can lead to disappointment if your princess turns out to be a drag queen! Be patient and weigh your odds, and you could save yourself from future embarrassment.

It is essential that you think about the art of seduction. Once you put your mind to it, you are a fabulous lover and partner. Insensitivity is your weakness—come on, you can transform yourself! You love lots of attention. But do this for your partner, too. Monitor how much attention you give your partner, particularly in terms of practical things (like washing the dishes). Believe it or not, if you put the effort into soothing your mate your sex life will improve a millionfold. One last thing: LISTEN. Put your effort into truly listening to your lover and sex will explode into everything you desired. It's simple! Just do it!

So, you fickle Arian lovers, what other star signs can match up to your impetuosity, high standards, and determination? The passionate, devoted Scorpio would be ideal or the fabulously romantic Sagittarius. Try the inexorable Libran or, if you like a bit of fire in your relationship, choose another Aries. If your lover is an Aries, don't drop gentle hints if you want something. Your lover is not mean but they do need things simply spelt out. And they'll thank you for it!

Famous Arian Lovers

Oh, Marlon Brando, where did it all go wrong? Brando is a typical **Arian boy**. He needs to be adored, he oozes buckets of charisma, and is **drop-dead gorgeous**. Brando is a warning to all Arians: Do you think you want it all? An island paradise? Hundreds of **dazzling beauties to adore you?** Any food and drink you desire? Every sexual exploit that you could possibly think of? Overindulgence, Aries style, can lead to Brando-size proportions **mentally, physically, and emotionally**. Even you supermen and superwomen can have too much of a good thing and burn out!

Wild Aries man Marlon Brando and Yvonne Doughty in The Wild One

THE PROS/THE CONS

The Pros You are generous, passionate, and prone to flamboyant expressions of feeling. You give your all and have a disarming, childlike charm that is capable of melting all hearts. You are so enthusiastic and irrepressible as a lover that you bring out the child in your partner as well. Who can deny you? When you are in good form, you are hilarious and romantic. You can always think up new ways to inspire your lover and usually do. When you are head over heels, you make your partner feel like the center of the universe and shower him or her with surprise gifts and all manner of unexpected delights.

The Cons You can be rather jealous and possessive while demanding freedom for yourself! You have a huge heart and a profound ability to love, but you can get caught up in selfish behavior and expect your partner to wait on you hand and foot. Your life tends to railroad others. You don't mean for this to happen, but you are the demanding child of the zodiac. When you want sex, you will stamp your foot until you get it. This is not the right attitude and can lead to explosive arguments. You expect to have all your partner's attention.

If You Want to Catch an Aries . . .

If it's a roller-coaster ride of love you're after, then this is the sign for you. Don't be daunted by an Arian's initial and scandalous self-appreciation. Arians are the babies of the zodiac and often use a bold approach to grab your attention before rolling over and showing you their soft underbelly.

These lovers like to play and will delight you with madcap antics and huge romantic gestures, all usually piled into the first few weeks. You may find yourself swept off your feet while being amazed by the sheer gall of these Arian hotheads.

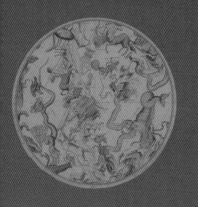

tAURUS

April 21 – May 21

STAR PROFILE

ELEMENT	Earth
KEY WORDS	Steady, committed, sensual, stubborn, reliable
ATTRACTED TO	Beauty, loyalty, homemakers, honesty, dependability, sensuality
RULER	Venus

You Taureans are naturally ahead in the game of love as your ruler is Venus, planet of love! Venus bestows on you all the qualities a lover desires, including sensuality, loyalty, and faithfulness. The Roman goddess Venus is equivalent to the Greek goddess Aphrodite. Venus is the sensual goddess of love, beauty, and pleasure. She has a deep passion for all of life's pleasures and all things beautiful. Venus bestows on you a love of beauty and a keen eye when it comes to art and interior design. She also gives you a love of expensive objects, a sensual nature, and a great connection with women, whatever your gender happens to be.

Secure Love

Your aim in life is emotional security. If you love someone, you will
give him or her 100 percent. You are stubborn and can be lazy,
driving your lover up the wall, but you also make him or her laugh
and enjoy the good things in life.

The longer you know someone the deeper your
love. Taureans hate letting go of past loves because
when you love, you love forever. Even after the
end of a relationship, you like to have
contact with your old partners.

You can also, however, be very
possessive, needing constant attention in
love. You would find it very hard to
tolerate your partner loving
anyone other than you,
including the cat! You have a
love for all things natural,
including animals. You need to
find balance in this area.

Zeus, god of the sky, created the
constellation of Taurus

The Mythology of Taurus

Legend has it that the chief Greek god Zeus disguised himself as a white bull. He used this technique to **seduce a beautiful young maiden** named Europa. When Zeus turned back into himself, he placed the bull **in the heavens**, creating the constellation Taurus.

In ancient Crete, the bull was a sacred creature, considered to be the **male manifestation** to complement the goddess. Priestesses performed acrobatics and vaulted over the charging bulls to **combine strength with grace**.

The good news is that when someone falls in love with you, they seem to fall under your spell and can never quite get you out of their system! With your earthy passion and delectable intimacy, you can reel in lovers, hook, line, and sinker. As a child of Venus you have a magical quality about you that is your birthright.

The Bull-Headed Taurean

You are an Earth sign, so of course you exude a rugged, down-to-earth nature that craves sensuality. Love and sex are closely tied for you, although you would not leave someone just because the sex had ended. Your commitment is practically guaranteed: You are one of the few star signs that truly thrives on commitment.

You are not called the bull for nothing! Certain parts of your temperament mirror this powerful creature, especially when in love. If someone rattles your cage, or worse, the cage of your partner, they will soon hear the scraping of the earth as you paw the ground and prepare to charge. You protect your partner with your life against any adversaries, real or imagined.

A typical Taurean might have the stamina of an ox, work full time, look after her baby, and cook buckets of good, wholesome food for her man. Being typically overindulgent, she also has the capacity to drink two bottles of wine and still run ten miles every morning, while writing two books.

Misfortune will certainly befall anyone who is rude or disrespectful to a Taurean, including his or her partner. Taureans will not hesitate to explain to their partner exactly what they are doing wrong, sometimes in a brutal fashion. Loyalty is the one thing you can be sure of with a Taurean partner. They may be able to criticize or nag you, but that is their domain alone.

You Taureans seek a mate who can turn your home into a love nest full of clean towels and ironed sheets. Home comforts bring out the best in you. Both male and female Taureans expect their mate to indulge them in this way. A Taurus woman will surround her mate with these wondrous things and a Taurus man will expect them. Taurean suitors can very easily get blissed-out by good food and fresh laundry!

Sex is one of the ways Taureans express love. You might spend hours snuggled up with your lover listening to music, as you lazily caress each other for hour upon hour. You have a strong need for passion. Because love and sex allow you to express your deeper feelings, you give your all and enjoy every aspect of sharing your love physically.

Routine is important to you and you need a partner who is equally predictable. Your needs must be met or you tend to feel very insecure and childlike. You suit a partner whom you can live with and rely on. You would hate to be involved with someone detached and independent, although most Taureans explore this kind of love at some point in their lives. You tend to forever bear the scars of the one that got away.

Marriage is your ideal state, or a relationship in which you are totally sure of your partner's devotion. In this you shine and find peace and happiness, for love is what makes your world go round. When you have a loyal partner, you are capable of anything. You work better and can achieve your high ideals. There is nothing more exquisite to you than security and long-lasting love.

When you trust, you trust completely. You will honor your partner all through the relationship; however, you find it very difficult to change. You can be set in your ways and have very strong opinions. Nothing can sway you once you have made up your mind about an issue. Your home is your castle and you love nothing better than to snuggle up with your loved one and watch television. You may have a hobby that takes you outside, which you stick to like clockwork, but home is where the heart is for you.

You don't give your heart cheaply, but wait for a worthy candidate to appear who fulfils your high expectations. You may test them for some time to make sure, perhaps for six months to a year. Then, as if by magic, they have all the commitment they desire. This technique works very well for you, as your chosen partner is relieved that you are finally theirs.

Avoid trying to control your partner (this can be a dangerous aspect of your personality that you should be aware of). Both of you have the right to be independent and unique individuals, so try not to morph the other person into another version of you. You do not want to be one of those eccentric couples that wear matching yellow warm-up suits and turquoise running shoes!

sex tip • sex tip •

Create a magical picnic, even if it's just in the garden. Food and the outdoors are a Taurean's dream. Grab some delicious homemade cakes, a bottle of bubbly, some baked chicken, and a large blanket. Find a secluded spot, as sex, food, and the outdoors will drive you crazy with ecstatic delight.

The TAUREAN MAN

You love overindulgence and sensuality. You need a woman who will enjoy staying home to eat and make love. You can be stubborn and appear like a huge immovable object, but in your favor, you are steady in your emotion and a damn good lover. You sulk like a little boy, but enjoy making up.

FAMOUS TAUREAN MEN
Salvador Dalí • Sigmund Freud • Al Pacino • Dante Gabriel Rossetti • William Shakespeare • George Clooney • Che Guevara

The TAUREAN WOMAN

You are strong and dependable and very sultry. You are great at back massages and sex in general. You have a voracious appetite for all-day lovemaking and all-night feasting and drinking. The longer you know your friends and lovers, the more you love them.

FAMOUS TAUREAN WOMEN
Evita Perón • Barbra Streisand • Cher
• Audrey Hepburn

Taurean woman Audrey Hepburn and Gregory Peck in the classic, romantic movie, Roman Holiday

Too Much of a Good Thing

A Taurus loves to overindulge. In fact, when you are in love, this tendency tends to triple. You may put on weight or get into a routine where all you do is eat, sleep, and make love! Although this sounds like good news, you find it depressing when you lose control. You also lose that sensuality when you pile on the pounds.

Being a dumpling is not your ideal state, because secretly you can be quite vain about your powerful and vigorous body. Getting out into the great outdoors with your lover can be the answer. You love nature and hiking and normally have a robust body and stamina. Make this kind of activity a regular event and both of you will feel much better.

The Bull is known for its mating abilities and prowess, but a bull that is cooped up in an enclosure, with no activity, soon loses its desire for life. Both female and male bulls adore physical exercise, but female Taureans need to have your "exercise" fit into your daily routine. If you can commit to this, your love life will benefit in all kinds of ways!

You Taureans love nothing more than indulging in sensual delights. Ruled by Venus, you can be quite demanding sexual partners. Sex is a need equivalent to food and water. Sex to you is an essential stress buster, and something to make a meal out of. Affection, such as lots of intimacy and touching, is an essential element to everyday life and you can wilt without it. Hot baths and getting a back rub after a long day at work will have you eating out of the palm of your partner's hand.

Cheating on a Bull

The kiss of death to a Taurean lover is dishonesty of any kind, especially infidelity. If you cheat on a Taurus, they will withdraw their love instantly. Once a Taurus has cut off from you, it's curtains. Like the proverbial elephant, the Bull does not forget. They may cling on for a while, for the sake of security, but in their heart you have lost them eternally.

If you love a Taurus, and want to keep your relationship with them, don't cheat on them under any circumstances, because they possess a sixth sense about love. If you are a Taurus reading this, you have probably underlined this part in red pen and left the page open for your spouse to see! Like a pig sniffing truffles, a Taurean can literally sniff out unfaithfulness. As a creature of the earth, you have a finely tuned animal-type sense about your partner.

If You Want to Catch a Taurus . . .

Taureans have a very acute sense of smell, so always find out what his or her favorite aftershave or perfume is and make an effort to wear it. They will spend hours sniffing your neck. Do not be alarmed by this animalistic behavior. Your scent—an aphrodisiac to the hot bull—will drive them crazy.

(Be warned that this can lead to armpit sniffing: I kid you not! Bulls can be very primal in their mating habits. Take it as a compliment. Whatever you do, try not to show alarm!)

Loyal Taurean woman ☛
Penelope Cruz at the
Academy Awards

Famous Taurean Lovers

Penelope Cruz is a classic example of a Taurean woman. Since her relationship started with the Cancer Tom Cruise, the two have been inseparable. It is thought that their relationship started as a friendship. Taureans can have a habit of falling in love with their friends, because that precious jewel—loyalty—is already established. Tom, as a Cancer, also likes and needs security. This gives this couple a chance of long-term prospects. Penelope Cruz played an ideal Taurean role in the film *Woman on Top*, in which she portrays a cook whose magical food made all men fall in love with her—although she is unable to stop loving her ex-husband. This is a great film to watch during a cozy night with your Taurean lover.

The PROS/The CONS

The Pros Loyal, committed, and sensual, you are an ideal partner. You love to be in love and shower your mate with loads of affection and cuddling. You explore sexuality with tenderness and stamina and will love your mate for all time. You love your lover more the longer you know them, and as the years pass your love increases. This is a gift anyone would be eager to share.

The Cons Lazy, obstinate, and pigheaded, you will never back down. You can be a bit unpleasant in criticizing your mate unnecessarily. Although you don't mean it, this can be very damaging. You dislike change and also expect your mate to stay the same, leaving little room for growth. Possessive, you can even resent your mate's friends and family.

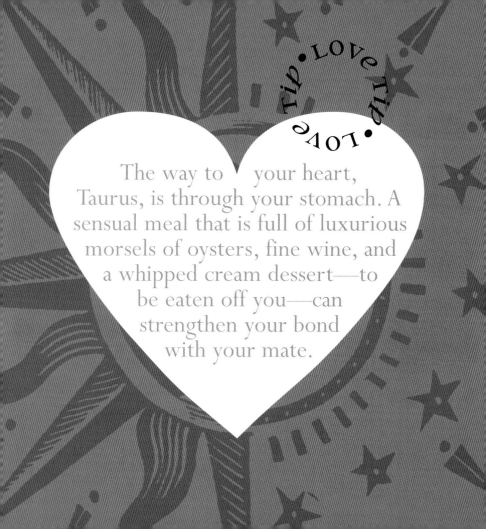

LOVE Tip • LOVE Tip • LOVE

The way to ♥ your heart,
Taurus, is through your stomach. A
sensual meal that is full of luxurious
morsels of oysters, fine wine, and
a whipped cream dessert—to
be eaten off you—can
strengthen your bond
with your mate.

gemiNi

May 22 – June 21

STAR PROFILE

ELEMENT	Air
KEY WORDS	Mercurial, changeable, unpredictable, intellectual
ATTRACTED TO	Intellect, brains, inspiring conversation, mental stimulation before passion
RULER	Mercury

You Geminis are curious creatures in love. Others find it hard to comprehend what inspires you. If someone can make you think and make you laugh, they are halfway to your heart. You adore good conversation and mental sparring. Love for you is a higher ideal— mental aerobics—not based on pure animal instinct.

Your passion needs to be varied and you can't stand routine in the bedroom. Love for you is an adventure, an exploration of unexplored territory, and you will stay with a lover who is inventive and unusual.

Sometimes you prefer a good book to sex and just adore discussing philosophy and politics. Your partner had better be well versed in numerous subjects if they are going to hold your interest.

The confusing thing about you as a lover—and don't try to deny it—is that you really are the twins! Some astrologers allude to one side of the twins being the "shadow side," a dark, mischievous sprite that causes mayhem just when those close to you relax. In reality, we all have a shadow side. Yours may just come to the surface more often than others!

In the Bedroom

Your ideal lover is someone who can transfix you with passionate conversations and surprise you—mundane is not for you. You are often drawn to eccentric types. Your friends may think you are crazy, but it is the mind that captivates you—not looks.

As a lover you have an unerring rapier wit. You will not tolerate confinement and are one of the few star signs who can happily handle nonmonogamous relationships (you can successfully separate aspects of your life, including lovers). This ethereal quality attracts lovers who are determined to pin you down. They don't stand a chance. Your flirtatious nature may ruffle a few feathers, but you were born to be free. You stay on your toes in a relationship and never give all of you, holding something back for yourself. But if you find a partner more intellectual, clever, or inspired than yourself, you will stay the course and be an eager student.

You love a good argument with your mate; not a heated, emotional one but balanced, detached debating. This can lead your partner to tear their hair out at your apparent lack of feeling, but feelings for you are sometimes inseparable from thought. You intrigue your loved one with your brilliant ideas and intellectual knowledge and you love to know what makes your partner tick.

The Mythology of Gemini

Castor and Pollux were a pair of twins whose father was Zeus. The twins had **many adventures together**, including saving Jason's boat (of Jason and the Golden Fleece) from sinking. When Castor eventually died, **Pollux was so saddened** that Zeus placed them both in the sky as the constellation of Gemini so they could be **together forever**.

Your mercurial energy makes you changeable; what is truth for you today may be fiction tomorrow. This chameleon air makes you a fascinating, if unstable, partner. You like to explore two sides of every issue. You are usually incredibly honest and charming and are never one to lie intentionally. You are intriguing, inspiring, witty, charming, talkative, inventive, and flexible. However, you are also fickle, easily bored, uncommitted, elusive, and unstable.

Your ideal lover is confident and successful, but not necessarily in a conventional sense. A mad artist or a poor poet might turn you on, or perhaps an inventor. You have a great natural ability to be successful at anything that you turn your hand to. Never one to be home every night, variety is the spice of life for you.

Twin Souls

The twin in you is often the split between your emotions and your thoughts. This is where the misunderstanding can begin. One day the emotional twin may appear and discuss long-repressed feelings. Your heart may open and for once all those emotions flow freely. The next day, moment, or second you are back to being detached. Unless you are with another sign linked to Mercury, like Virgo, this is sometimes impossible to understand.

You might think about keeping a journal of your feelings to monitor exactly what comes up in times of emotional freedom. How do your mood swings affect your sexual performance? Don't be tempted to use this as a tool to dissect and analyze! If you really need to do that, keep two journals to express these different sides. This can give you clarity, and can also give you something concrete to share with your loved one.

LOVE•Tip•LOVE•Tip•LOVE

Gemini, your reality may be very different from that of anyone else you know. Ask your partner to handle your emotions gently, even if you appear to be totally irrational. Your partner should know that if you cut them off, they should never cause a scene. If your partner makes a fuss or throws a tantrum, you will disappear in a flash. If you, in your mercurial way, end your relationship out of the blue, your partner needs to back off and tell you that they understand so as to give you the space to reconsider. You Geminis love communication, but you don't understand loss of emotional control.

The Gemini Man

Intelligent and talkative, you have a brilliant mind. You will capture your partner with your knowledge and charm, but you can be very difficult to tie down. You rush through life like a mad professor on your way to a Nobel Prize. Sexually you like to give and receive and can be quite inventive. You need your partner to communicate her sexual desires verbally, as this puts you at ease. You are a bit of a social butterfly and are always late. If your partner gets into your head, she is sure to get into your pants!

FAMOUS GEMINI MEN
Johnny Depp • Bob Dylan • Boy George • Morgan Freeman • John F. Kennedy

The Gemini Woman

A genius at many things, the Gemini mind is faster than a speeding bullet. You do not suffer fools gladly and adore those with different views. You are sexy and can display boyishness and ultrafemininity. This is your gift: to be diverse in yourself and to help your partner get in touch with their own diversity. You are attracted to what is in your partner's head rather than what he looks like, and you need constant challenges to maintain a long-term relationship. Sexually you are curious and can be attracted to both men and women.

FAMOUS GEMINI WOMEN
Anne Frank • Liz Hurley • Angelina Jolie • Kylie Minogue • Marilyn Monroe • Joan Rivers

Sexy Gemini Marilyn Monroe, with her playwright husband, Arthur Miller

Gemini: Now You See Her, Now You Don't!

You often get a bad rap in astrology because of your alleged "here today, gone tomorrow" fickleness. Come on, admit it! There have been times in your life when you have loved passionately and all the sexual vibes were right. You were committed, happy even, and then one day you woke up and right out of the blue it was over. You couldn't explain why. It was time to move on.

This Gemini trait of leaving a sexual partner unexpectedly after a period of time does have an element of truth to it. It could take weeks, months, or in some cases twenty-five years, but this alarming and seemingly irrational detachment can occur, often without warning. The good news for you is that it gives you clear opportunities to reinvent yourself and find yourself in a new life. You never look back but start again with the enthusiasm of a child.

Sex for the Gemini can be quite complex. As in all areas, you find it difficult to make your mind up about which kind of sex you actually desire. A surefire bet with the ethereal Gemini is to have soft, stroking, and gentle "cosmic sex." Sex for you is a deeper level of communication. But you need the soft, ethereal, sweeping strokes and gentle slow kisses to be really fulfilled. You love to look deeply into your partner's eyes and float off on a cloud of sensuality.

Tell your lover to take you to a place you've never been to and never thought of! Try a trip to a science museum, a talk on ancient philosophy, or a wacky class on how to be a stand-up comic. Finish up in an unusual or obscure restaurant where you ask your partner to pretend you are meeting for the first time, both of you coming up with a whole new make-believe identity. This should blow you unpredictable and unusual Geminis away! It will be like having sex for the first time again and again!

Famous Gemini Lovers

Johnny Depp has been branded as a bit of a **wild man** when it comes to his love life. He had a tempestuous relationship with Winona Ryder—a stubborn and tenacious Capricorn—that involved many break-ups and make-ups. Johnny seems to like **unpredictable women** and as a Gemini he is easily **bored**. His lover needs to be on her toes to keep him emotionally and sexually engaged. After Winona came Kate Moss—a no-nonsense Scorpio—and the passionate, roller coaster style of relationship continued. Now Johnny seems to finally have **settled down** with Vanessa Paradis—another **stubborn Capricorn**—who will have a grounding influence. The pair currently have two children and seem very stable.

Wild Gemini lover Johnny Depp ☞

Gemini fickle- ness can be
irritating for any partner. As much as
they need to understand you, you need to
make them feel extra special—particularly
after those inevitable misunderstandings.
You naturally show your love and
enjoy giving little gifts, but give
your partner lots of your
time, with extra hugs
and kisses, to renew
their faith
in you.

The PROS/The CONS

The Pros Your partners will be astounded by the variety of knowledge and wit you sassy lovers have. You will entertain and beguile your lover, and teach them a lot along the way, including (no doubt) new sexual techniques and the art of exploring their mind as a sexual organ!

The Cons Unpredictable and elusive, you mercurial Geminis are highly changeable. You can never guarantee that you won't change your mind or switch your point of view right at the last moment. You are easily bored and can leave your partner feeling dull as dishwater. Insecure partners should steer well clear of Geminis.

CANCER

June 22 – July 22

STAR PROFILE

ELEMENT	Water
KEY WORDS	Nurturing, maternal, loving, evasive, emotional
ATTRACTED TO	Stability, family, structure, security
RULER	The Moon

What a wondrous contradiction you are! You are such a sensitive soul masquerading as a warrior with that hard outer shell. You look impervious to the rough and tumble of life.

Anyone who cares to get to know you for longer than five minutes will surely see beneath that lame disguise. It has to be said: You don't always make it easy for yourself! Like the crab, you scoot sideways to get to your goal, and in love you are no different.

Cancers are ruled by the Moon, and can therefore be very emotional. You are constantly craving a safe harbor in which to lay down your anchor. Sex for you is a sacred act, a mating ritual to be danced only with a true love. You are the mother of the zodiac and as such you seek a secure partner. There are two things that you see as sacred to you: the home and children.

Whether you are male or female, you have a delicious nurturing quality about you and a deep love for children. Often Cancers have big issues with their own mothers and seek to play this out in a relationship. Both genders have the strongest desire to be parents, and what excellent parents you make.

The thing is, this underlying desire for security and roots can manifest itself even on a first date. No superficial dating for you! You want it all and often feel you haven't got time to waste. If your date screws up or offends your delicate. sensibilities during the first course, you're out of that restaurant and back to your favorite place— home—rather than waste any more precious time. You do this in the nicest possible way, of course, because you don't like to hurt another's feelings (you're likely to pretend that you've had a call from your Aunt Madge, and she needs your help to find her beloved canary, which has tragically flown the coop!)

You are very sensitive to others' needs and can listen to others' problems for hours on end, caring and looking after them. You are a giver in that way and see it as your duty to be compassionate and secure for every waif and

Artemis, also Diana, goddess of the Moon

The Mythology of Cancer

The crab, Cancer, was ordered by Hera (Greek Goddess of the hearth and jealous wife of Zeus) to destroy Hercules, (one of Zeus's many children). While he was in a battle with the multiheaded water snake Hydra, Cancer pinched the toe of Hercules. The crab clung on, wanting to distract Hercules and cause him to be killed. Hercules found this extremely annoying and squashed the persistent crab to death. Hera placed Cancer in the sky for his dedication. This didn't really do a lot of good for the crab, but immortality is great status! Cancers still sometimes personify this myth by being tenacious, and never knowing when it is time to let go.

stray that comes along, including your partner. Watch out for that crushing and tedious martyr syndrome that can predominate in a Cancer personality. It is not attractive and doesn't do you justice. You are a child of the Moon and worth more than that!

If you do not express your own needs in a long-term relationship (which you find particularly difficult to do), you can find yourself becoming bitter or manipulative. Walking sideways to achieve your end result has given you a bad reputation, astro-logically, and you have been accused of being moody and unreasonable. You can be a real cantankerous, crabby, critical crustacean when you want to be! The reason for this is that you can suffer from a lack of belief in yourself and a deep, inner insecurity that may have plagued you all your life.

One of your lessons here on Earth is to overcome this, and preferably within a relationship. Your partners end up needing you because you mother them and do everything for them. Both of you can end up resenting this, so it is wise to express up front what you would like from the relationship.

You often play games when starting a relationship, not only to test your new mate but also to capture them completely. What you need to realize is that you are lovable as you are, and you don't need to become elusive or indispensable to get your heart's desire.

Place a crystal under running water and visualize it being cleansed of any previous vibrations. Repeat this with a white candle. As a child of the Moon, you have a magical quality about you. At the full moon, find a place outside where you can see the Moon or find a window that looks outside. Rub some lavender oil on your white candle, and as you stare at the full Moon visualize her powerful rays bathing you in cleansing moonlight. As the rays pour down over you, feel all insecurity being washed away. Feel the Moon energy replenishing you with an inner confidence. Place the moonstone or clear quartz on the windowsill or outside for three days to "capture" the Moon's energy.

The CANCER MAN

You are sensitive and sweet, and you respect women. You hate loud arguments and will do anything to keep the peace. You need to discuss your emotions more than most or you can get resentful. You are the ideal parent and love kids. You're a sensitive lover and will put your partner's needs before your own. If your partner treats you with kindness, this will help your mood swings; you feel things so very deeply and need reassurance. Underneath your confident exterior lies a gentle soul unsure of your abilities.

FAMOUS CANCERIAN MEN
Tom Cruise • Tom Hanks • Nelson Mandela • Paul McCartney • O. J. Simpson • Mike Tyson • Robin Williams

The CANCER WOMAN

As the perfect mother and homemaker, you take care of everyone. The best cook of all the star signs, you love to nurture your partner. You love romance and all things feminine. Even you career Cancer women know how to look after your partners. If you try to ignore this side of yourself, it will come out eventually. You are magical and kind, but often scuttle sideways to avoid confrontation. Over the years this can lead to a huge blowout, with all those stored-up slights getting hurled in your partner's face. Communication and gentleness will enhance the relationship.

FAMOUS CANCERIAN WOMEN
Pamela Anderson • Diana, Princess of Wales • Anjelica Huston • Camilla Parker Bowles • Ginger Rogers • Jane Russell • Meryl Streep

The Crab in the Bedroom

Sex for you can be accompanied by a bit of guilt. You naturally associate sex with babies, and if you are a Cancer woman, you usually have issues about fertility. Cancer women seem to have an extreme reaction to the procreation process, either getting pregnant at the drop of a hat or taking much longer than usual. This can lead to an obsession with all things related to getting pregnant or to an avoidance of pregnancy. Chill out and relax, and your concerns will evaporate. You are a naturally sexual being; your body was made for love. If you are a woman, you are curvy or give the illusion of being curvy. Your sensuality can be spotted for miles. If you are a guy, you have a tenderness about you that drives women wild, and you are usually aware of your female side and get along tremendously well with women.

This natural sensuality is one of your biggest assets. If you think about it, you'll realize that a part of you knows this! You will probably have big, watery, emotional eyes that reveal the depths of your feelings. Those eyes also express empathy for friends and partners and make people feel safe. Turn this amazing lovingness you have onto yourself and you will blossom. Your insecurity is your only enemy. You are loved, so come out of that shell and shine. When given responsibility in work or love, you will do your utmost to fulfill it. Why not make that commitment to yourself?

If you are a woman, you may have exceptional breasts; if you are a man, you may adore breasts. This is all part of your nurturing sexuality. You are thrilled when a lover is tender with you and shows you that they care. If they nurture you, you will do anything for them. However, if they stamp on your feelings, you just might pinch them with your claws while retreating sideways. Communicate this rather than retaliating: You don't want to end up handling things like your water brother Scorpio!

The Crab in His Shell

Cancers, if you want to become excited, sexually and emotionally, an evening at home with a home-cooked meal, surrounded by your family is, ironically, the answer. Your partner can arouse your feelings and make you forever theirs, if they take the time to ensure that you feel secure, safe, and, most of all, appreciated. If your partner supplies these few simple things, you will adore, worship, and look after them for the rest of your lives. If your partner shows a maternal or paternal side, the secure feeling that this gives means that you can't wait to get them into the bedroom.

Famous Cancer Lovers

Princess Diana has to be the most famous Cancer woman. She manifested all the external signs of being a Cancer Moon goddess. This was reflected in **her sensitivity, her love for her children**, and her commitment to Charles (a Scorpio)—even during media allegations of his affair. Her Cancerian sign could also be seen in her romantic **affair with James Hewitt**. James would have had a very Piscean energy, and his **romantic and sensitive** side would have **been attractive**. Dodi Fayed—her last amour—was an Aries and probably made Diana feel safe because Arian men can often be considered masculine. This type of partner tends to appeal to an ultrafeminine Cancer.

Sensitive Cancerian Lady Diana on her wedding day ☛

sex tip • sex tip •

In sexual relationships you will not let a matter rest if you think you are right. You often end up under your partner's stiletto or boot heel as they escape by trampling over your insecure and tenacious martyrdom. To counter this reaction, try this with your partner. Many of you are alleged to have a slightly subservient side sexually, and many of you love to be dominated or to experience being taken by a more forceful lover. We are not talking about something terrible here—just the desire to be able to abandon yourself sexually while your partner takes control. This is about power, not pain, and the turn-on to the Cancer is the symbolic release. Allow your partner to gently tie you to the bed with silk scarves while they tease you sexually with gentle caresses and steamy foreplay.

The PROS/The CONS

The Pros You supremely love and create the perfect home. You have a wicked sense of humor and have all your guests—as well as your partner—in stitches. You exude a warmth and lovingness that is hard to beat. You have a god or a goddess feel about you and are very benevolent when you want to make your partner feel like a king or queen. You ooze sexiness and were born to mate. In so many ways you are the dream partner. Don't let that lack of belief let you down: What we believe, we create!

The Cons You have a dramatic flair that can be used to make relationships fantastically fun. However, if you are in one of your emotional moods, you can use this drama in a negative way, clinging to your partner's shoes with that huge pincer as he or she tries to leave the house for an evening class. Don't you know that when you are confident and elegant and all the other fabulous things you are, they wouldn't want to leave the house anyway? But we all need a little freedom—especially you— to dream and create, to sit and watch the Moon. Insecurity within a relationship is your weak point and this can be very draining for you and the other person. Believe in yourself, because you truly are wonderful.

leo

July 23 – August 22

STAR pROFile

ELEMENT	Fire
KEY WORDS	Charismatic, regal, proud, assertive, gorgeous
ATTRACTED TO	Beauty, looks, success, adoration, spirit
RULER	The Sun

Ah, Leo, you gorgeous, irresistible creature! In love you are a joy to behold. But only as long as you are adored and caught in the right mood (that makes you glow).

You are not one to suffer fools gladly—in or out of love—and you have extremely high standards. In the bedroom department you never get any complaints! Your lover, for one, wouldn't dare complain, because they would be hitting the sidewalk with all of their belongings before they knew what had hit them!

A Leo in a state of passion is hard to beat. This is because making love is the ultimate stress-buster for you and you are remarkably good at it. You like to be the boss, however, and do what pleases you . . . unless you are trying to hunt a new mate, in which case you will do whatever it takes to prove what a perfect lover you are. You will try anything once and it often appears easy.

When you walk into a room you have the regal charisma of the lion, oozing crackling sex appeal in a lofty, majestic way.

No matter what the style, you are guaranteed to dress appropriately every time. You are totally hip. It is extremely unusual to see a badly dressed Leo—you can make a pair of fleecy pajamas look glamorous. As a lover you purr with desire. All aspects of the sexual process drive you crazy. You love passion: You were born to be a lover and don't you just know it! As in most things you have to be the best. You are proud and need constant praise for your outstanding sexual performance.

Primping the Lion's Mane

Your biggest difficulty in love is that you base a lot of your attractions not only on chemistry and achievement, but also on looks—as long as your partner is not as good-looking as you, of course! You have to have a partner with the "star" factor. No wilting lilies for you, unless you are that very rare creature, the insecure Leo. That unusual breed of Leo is attracted to "yes" people.

You proceed to place your mate on a pedestal and only want a lover you can be truly proud of. This can blind you to reality, because like all fire signs you have an element of naïveté. If you love your partner, you think they must be perfect. On top of that,

The Mythology of Leo

The Greeks had a bit of an unfortunate myth for Leo. Hercules was set the task of **killing an invincible lion** that terrorized the hills around Nemean. This lion, like you, Leo, was immune to weapons and had won every fight . . . until, of course, he met Hercules! Hercules wrestled the lion to death and then **wore his hide for protection.** The moral of this story may be that no one, **not even you**, Leo, is invincible.

they must always think that you are perfect as well. You absolutely detest disapproval from a loved one.

You are generous to a fault and share all that you have with a partner, but he or she must have impeccable manners. If someone is rude or coarse (outside the bedroom), you will give them one of your famous, withering royal looks.

Leos in Love

In the beginning of a relationship you are suave, dignified, charming, and extremely attentive. Outside relationships you are used to being worshiped and getting your own way. Madonna is a prime example of a Leo woman. No matter what criticism or difficulties she's had, she's bounced back to conquer the world. This incredible sense of self-belief, however, doesn't always translate to the way Leos act when they are in love. This is when the soft underbelly of you big cats starts to show. The good news is that you will only bow down for so long, as you quickly get bored with being subservient. It is not in your nature and you subsequently find that you had the power all along.

The worst thing that your lover could ever do to you is disrespect you or try to break your spirit. Leos need a partner who supports them and boosts that infinite ego. You really are pussycats in love and you need a mate to be your rock. All that arrogance is just a cover-up to mask your vulnerability.

You know what you want and you'll get it. Even the people who say, "Who the hell does he think he is?" secretly admire or are jealous of the quiet self-assurance of the magnificent Leo. Just deal with these mere mortals with your usual magnanimous warmth.

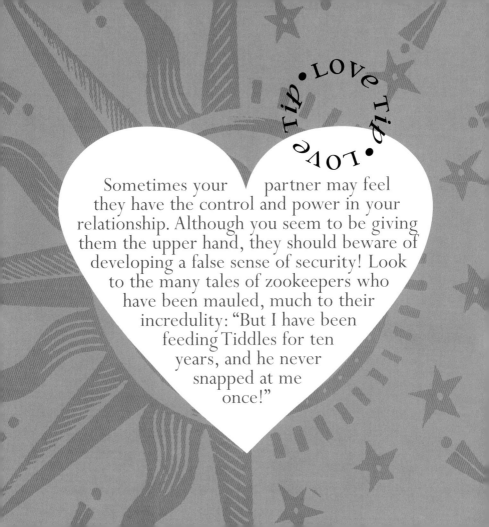

LOVE Tip • LOVE Tip • LOVE Tip •

Sometimes your partner may feel they have the control and power in your relationship. Although you seem to be giving them the upper hand, they should beware of developing a false sense of security! Look to the many tales of zookeepers who have been mauled, much to their incredulity: "But I have been feeding Tiddles for ten years, and he never snapped at me once!"

The Leo Man

You are the king of the jungle and expect to be treated that way. Proud and somewhat vain, you preen in front of the mirror as much as women do. You expect your partner to tell you how gorgeous you are and to behave as if you were a love god. You are a good lover because you don't like to fail at anything. Seeing that your partner has pleasure makes you feel even better about yourself. You are sexy and have an aura of sexiness that is difficult to deny. You will, however, allow anyone to adore you, so your partner should always make the effort with you or you will pad off to the next lioness.

FAMOUS LEO MEN
Ben Affleck • Bill Clinton • Robert De Niro • Alfred Hitchcock • Dustin Hoffman • Mick Jagger • Carl Jung • Wesley Snipes • Andy Warhol

The Leo Woman

What an exceptionally stunning woman you are! When you walk into a room everyone senses you. You are elegant and sexy without even trying. Men love you and women want to be you. Your taste and smell are flawless. You like to play cat and mouse with men and command respect. You love a difficult lover even though you won't admit this. In bed you are a real panther and can scare the pants off most men. You adore raw sex, so your partner should go with you and enjoy it. You are a once-in-a-lifetime experience.

FAMOUS LEO WOMEN
Sandra Bullock • Coco Chanel • Mata Hari •
Whitney Houston • Jacqueline Kennedy •
Jennifer Lopez • Madonna

*Leo man Dustin Hoffman
with Susan George while
filming* Straw Dogs

King of the Bedroom

In relationships pride can be a bit of a problem. You don't like to back down and can be quite demanding both sexually and emotionally. You quickly lose your respect for people who lie, cheat, or are superficial. You need to be the center of attention, especially in bed.

Your partner needs to know that you have a very clear idea about what you want and, if you don't get it, you can be quite scathing. If your lover's sexual performance is lacking, you can be a little uncompromising in your response. To roar that a loved one is crap in bed in the middle of the act of coitus is not likely to win friends and influence people! Your lover will become so nervous they will never be able to perform and satisfy you! Female Leos are particularly known for this kind of direct approach.

You will never catch a Leo lover humoring you in the bedroom, and the partners of Leos are likely to get a very direct appraisal of their sexual skills (or lack of them). Leos need to tread a bit gently and be kind, and they will get better results from their loved one.

One of the naughty fantasies you have is to film your act of passion with your partner. You also love to look at yourself when making love and probably enjoy lovemaking by a mirror. Some people may see you as vain, but so what! You are proud of yourself and that is a good thing. Even a Leo who may appear to be unattractive at first glance oozes charisma and becomes beautiful.

You Leos love to socialize with your partners and show them off, as you are always proud of whom you are with or you wouldn't go out with them. Some of you very naughty Leos have a lover on the side who you don't feel is quite good enough, and so will never be caught dead with them outside the bedroom. This arrogance has given you a bad name, and also is not good karma! We are all equal and, if you are going to have sex with someone in the first place, it is important for you to honor them. You do not do this with malicious intent, but could leave some very damaged lovers behind if you are not more careful. You would be mortified if you knew you caused them pain, but it is just your natural inner confidence that causes you to act this way.

Lions of the Social World

One only has to look at the list of Leo celebrities to know how exceptional and glamorous you Leos are. Coco Chanel is a prime example of a smart, beautiful, razor-sharp Leo. Her elegance and beauty—which made her fortune—were sought after and emulated by the entire world. Coco grew up in poverty and her mother died of malnutrition, but like a typical lioness she proved to be unstoppable.

Lots of Leos are so fiercely independent that they do not settle down in a relationship until late in life, if they settle down at all. Coco Chanel never married; Madonna has found happiness quite late in life; and Mick Jagger has always been a free spirit with an unconventional love life. This strong sense of self runs very deep, and it is almost impossible to tame your Leo lover. Ultimately, they will always call the shots.

Dress up in your glad rags and make your partner take you out to the trendiest place in town. You love bragging to friends about this kind of thing, and will love the fact that your partner took you there. Make sure that they give you enough warning, however, so you can get spruced up. When you get home, have your partner pour you your favorite drink, turn on some slow music, and give you a sexy strip show. You'll love this, as you'll feel like a real king or queen watching them perform just for you.

Famous Leo Lovers

Jacqueline Kennedy is the epitome of a lover and a Leo woman. She is elegant, charismatic, **stunning**, and as a result, found herself with the **two most powerful husbands** in the world.

John F. Kennedy, a Gemini, would have appealed to any Leo. When he became the president of the United States, **Jackie Kennedy became the perfect president's wife**. She was worshiped by the world for her class and style. Throughout allegations of John F.

Kennedy's womanizing, Jackie never lost face. She responded to his alleged affairs with dignity, but one could imagine in private that her Leo personality **was not pleased**. The worst thing that you can do to a Leo is to humiliate them. However, JFK was lucky enough to hold on to this lovely Leo asset, and Jackie went on to be **adored by a whole nation** and considered to be American royalty. Her amazing bravery at his side during his assassination won her an award.

Her next lover after JFK's assassination was Aristotle Onassis. Onassis came from one of the **most powerful and richest families in the world**. Jackie the lioness knew how to pick 'em! Both men caused her heartache, but she never gave up and is still remembered today as the best-loved First Lady in the United States.

Always elegant Leo Jackie Kennedy

To connect with your partner on a deeper level, try a heart orgasm. Sit facing each other and rest your hands on one another's hearts. Imagine your heart opening like a flower, from bud to bloom. As you look into your partner's eyes, say, "I welcome and honor your soul." Remember to close your heart back down when you are done.

The PROS/The CONS

The Pros Gorgeous and great to be seen with, you will sweep your partner off their feet. You are alluring and irritatingly good at whatever you do, including making love! You will adore your partner and give them your very soul if committed. Glamorous and charming, you will make your lover feel like a million bucks.

The Cons You arrogant, furry felines can spend more time looking in the mirror at yourselves than at your lover. The world has to revolve around what pleases you, and if your love doesn't give you enough attention, you are off to richer hunting grounds.

ViRgo

August 23 – September 22

STAR PROFILE

ELEMENT	Earth
KEY WORDS	Picky, perfectionist, detailed, erotic, hidden, enigma, celibate, base
ATTRACTED TO	Wealthy, successful, strong, unobtainable, charismatic
RULER	Mercury

Hello, Virgo! To the outside world, and even to yourself sometimes, you may appear to be the virgin. Butter wouldn't melt in your perfect mouth. You are the good girl or boy of the zodiac and are said to see sex and passion as something quite distasteful. Ha! That's not entirely accurate, is it?

Almost all Virgos have two sides to their personality: the virgin and the vixen. Whether you are male or female, young or old, the two sides of the Virgo can be seen. The thing about being extreme (and you allegedly have a more extreme nature than most other signs) is that the more you suppress one side of yourself, the stronger the other side becomes!

The Virgin and the Sacred Whore

The Vestal Virgins, who are connected with your sign, were dedicated to Vesta, the Roman goddess of the home and hearth. There is a tendency for you to shy away from sex once you are married so it is important to watch out for any dip in libido in long-term relationships. You become more engrossed in making the home a functional and perfect place to be, and can get caught up in the detail of life rather than living in the present.

Interestingly enough, your connection with the Virgin may not be all that it appears to be. In ancient Sumeria—one of the world's earliest civilizations—virgin meant "belonging to no man." Virgins were strong, independent women who were free to sleep with whom they wanted, or were sacred prostitutes—women who slept with the men that came to the temple, and who were thought to literally become the goddess during lovemaking.

These sacred, sexual creatures were highly thought of and had to be pleasured sexually first. It was one of the highest honors to become a sacred prostitute, and perhaps this apparent contradiction in your nature stems from here. Sex for you swings between these two extremes. If you can harness it so that it can be adventurous yet pure, you've got a winner.

The Mythology of Virgo

Virgo is a goddess constellation called Astraea. She is known as the goddess of virtue and justice, and is a daughter of Zeus. Interestingly, she is linked to Pandora, who opened the box that let out all manner of corruption upon Earth. When this happened, the gods had to escape to the heavens. Astraea was the last to leave, and is still said to be waiting for Earth to become "perfect" again so she can return.

Astraea seems to have a lot in common with you, Virgo. The moral of this story is don't hang around for things to turn out perfectly! Act now and enjoy life. Because you also embody the minxlike qualities of Pandora, and secretly enjoy a bit of mischief, you really are a fun person!

A Sexual Dilemma

You are the original Ms. (or Mr.) Moneypenny: Beneath that crisp and precise appearance lies a wild volcano of love. The difficulty for your lover is to know when you are feeling raunchy and naughty, and when you are in your prim and proper Virgin mode. Misfortune will befall the lover who tries to get down and dirty with you when you are not in Vixen mode.

For you, the first step in becoming a great and balanced lover is accepting this very real dichotomy. Some Virgos live out extremes, enjoying a lifestyle based on exploring their fantasies and indulging their imaginative side, ignoring their delicate and pure spirit. However, don't feel you can't enjoy this—just don't dedicate yourself to it. You Virgos always seem to have a touch of guilt and may feel a little lost if you rebel in this way. You are a steamy, passionate creature and it is healthy to admit it. Celebrate that distinctive sensual side, because it is a big part of you.

Communication may be challenging for you as a lover, but you will be rewarded if you find a partner with whom you can share all sides of yourself. When you find your balance you are an ideal lover. Tantric sex would suit you, because the concept of communication through spiritual sex really turns you on.

LOVE Tip • LOVE Tip • LOVE

In order to seduce you, your partner
has to treat you as though you are pure
and allow you to slowly open up to their
courtly advances. If your partner holds
back a bit, you will come forward.
Your standoffishness will pass with
time. Your partner should bring
you little treats and presents,
but avoid grand gestures
until they are
sure of your
feelings.

the virgo man

You can be a little tedious sometimes, as you have very set views on how a woman should be. You don't mean to criticize, and also don't realize you are causing offense, but your perfectionist ways may drive your lover bananas. When you let your hair down, you can be as unconventional as you are conventional. No doubt you have some very kinky fantasies indeed, if your partner can get to the bottom of your passion. You may have a hobby you are crazy about. You are a creature of habit: If your lover gets you into the habit of spending time with her, who knows what may happen?

FAMOUS VIRGO MEN
Sean Connery • Michael Jackson • Stephen King •
D. H. Lawrence • Keanu Reeves

The Virgo Woman

You are hardworking and meticulous in your appearance, but you really do fantasize about getting down and dirty. You are a secret romantic—no matter what you pretend in public—and crave the perfect lover. As this perfect lover doesn't exist, your partner will have to do!

You Virgo women often feel badly about yourselves and it is your partner's job to adore you. Once you feel safe and loved you will reward your partner in ways that will make his eyes water. You have a strong and passionate love beneath the practical exterior and are just waiting for someone to unearth it. How exciting!

FAMOUS VIRGO WOMEN
Lauren Bacall • Ingrid Bergman • Jacqueline Bisset •
Cameron Diaz • Queen Elizabeth I • Greta Garbo •
Sophia Loren • Mother Teresa • Shania Twain

Sensual Virgo

You can devour your lover and pleasure them beyond belief, but everything must be perfect or you will lose interest. You also have a very strong sense of smell and cannot abide uncleanliness. You are meticulous with personal hygeine, and would ideally like your partner to have a bath or shower before you hit the sack.

Getting to know the difference between what is in your head and what you would like to be in reality can be tricky for you. You get confused and perhaps don't realize that some fantasies are better left unrealized, while others are fabulous to explore. Give guilt a kick in the pants and allow yourself to let your imagination go wild. When you do reveal all of yourself to your lover, they are in for a real treat.

Everyone has fantasies. Usually they wouldn't dream of acting them out, nor would they want to. But humans seem to be somewhat conditioned to fantasize about what they are not supposed to desire. This is the human dilemma, and anyone who pretends to think only of white sheets, log fires, and their current partner, is almost certainly telling lies! Relax and accept yourself as the diverse and perfect human being you are. Your perfection is made up of all the unique imperfections that make you who you are!

🐦 *Passionate Virgo Sean Connery, in* You Only Live Twice

Famous Virgo Lovers

One only has to look at Lauren Bacall to see how fabulous a Virgo can be as a committed lover. Her **enduring and complete adoration for Capricorn** Humphrey Bogart is the love that legends are made of. They were the **ideal couple** in lots of ways, even though Bacall allegedly had **an affair with Bogart** while he was still married (perhaps expressing the other extreme of her nature). Lauren Bacall soon became the ideal wife and mother and they **lived happily together** until his tragic, early death.

It is interesting to note, however, that you can also find **famous Virgo virgins**, including Queen Elizabeth I and Mother Teresa.

Virgo woman Lauren Bacall and her loving husband, Humphrey Bogart

The PROS/The CONS

The Pros You have the capacity to venture where no other will. Beneath that composed exterior is a tiger of love waiting to be unleashed. When you truly let go sexually, wild abandon swiftly follows. Nothing is taboo to you when you are on a roll. The more sensual and earthy, the better you like it. You will also iron your lover's shirt perfectly and keep their bills, clothes, and life in order. You strive in yourself to be the perfect partner.

The Cons When you are expressing your more reserved side, you can be hell as a lover! You can be controlling, celibate, and never happy. If your lover gets on your bad side, they won't get any love! At times you may shy away from sex for months and expect your partner to be perfectly happy with this. You may well disapprove of certain aspects of your partner's nature, as you can have a very fixed view of how things should be. At worst, your lover should expect no sex and loads of criticism.

Role-play with your lover that you are a god or a goddess. Let your partner bathe you in a bath of milk and honey and dry you with freshly laundered towels. Place a large white sheet on the floor or bed strewn with different colored flower petals. Surround this with big bowls of grapes so your lover can feed you, and also with lots of big altar candles (be careful with these). Have a large bowl of olive oil mixed with ylang-ylang and rose oil, and allow yourself to be massaged from head to foot before being made love to in your favorite way with you commanding the foreplay.

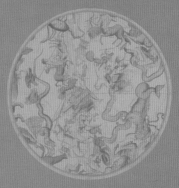

1ibRA

September 23 – October 23

STAR PROFILE

ELEMENT	Air
KEY WORDS	Justice, love, charm, balance, moods
ATTRACTED TO	Charm, vulnerability, intellectuals, creative, careers
RULER	Venus

Sex and love go hand in hand for Libran lovers. Your scales indicate that you need the balance of love and sex in order to be truly fulfilled. Libra is supposed to be the sign of relationships, and particularly of marriage. Once you Librans are in a secure relationship, you can practice and grow sexually. You can explore your passion, inch by inch, slowly but surely.

Like the other air signs—Gemini and Aquarius—a certain amount of mental stimulation must precede the sexual act for you to be turned on. You are definitely not a "wham, bam, thank-you-ma'am" kind of guy or girl. The way to your sensual side is through your mind. This is your biggest sex organ and it is unlimited! You

love to be seduced with the voice and can enjoy talking through the act of passion, much to the surprise of your lovers! (Unless, of course, they are an air sign as well.)

Generally you are quite shy and are not at all pushy, unlike your opposite—Aries—who rushes in where angels fear to tread. Your seduction technique is very slow and subtle. You dream of a lover who can understand your delicate personality, but are unaware that sometimes you can be very moody and unpredictable, so it's hard for them to keep up with your feelings! Unfortunately, your scales are very rarely perfectly balanced.

You can often enjoy spending time alone and, even when in a passionate relationship, you need quiet times to be able to reflect. You spend hours pondering upon life and even more time trying to make decisions. The act of love can often be a bit of a slow starter for you, and many Librans remain innocent of the joys of love until they become a bit older.

Very loyal and loving, the Libran man will be ready to serve his woman as long as she needs him. However, Libran men can sometimes seek a sexual partner who is stronger than they are and who knows what her man wants. On the other hand, a Libran woman likes a strong man who understands that his mate likes to enjoy her individuality and freedom.

Pursue Your Own Pleasure

One interesting thing about you Librans is that you can sometimes get more turned on giving pleasure than receiving it. You have a big heart and are the least selfish lover of the zodiac. Yes, you can be shy, but once you know what your lover wants and what arouses them, you are eager to please.

You can be a bit prudish like Virgo, but if someone verbalizes to you what excites them, you can be persuaded to experiment. The idea, however, must come from the other person, as you wouldn't like to lead astray. Although this is your natural instinct (and you are less likely to have the Virgo, two-sided extreme of virgin or whore sexuality), it really would be a good idea to let your hair down and discover what truly turns you on. Your mind, like all the rest of the air signs, is filled with sexual fantasies and you are always exploring them in the privacy of your own head. Perhaps it would be good to put that vivid imagination to use. You are also very easily bored in relationships, but are generally loyal enough to stay the course.

You are one of the few signs that can truly live with celibacy, and you may have experienced long periods of time when you weren't sexual. However, because one of your key lessons is partnership, you often have intense friendships or business partnerships during these periods when you give all of your time and energy to another person. When you are hooked into a passionate relationship, you love to be romantic and write love letters or show your love through little gifts. You tend to be quite practical as well and may even make unusual gifts for your partner. This charming aspect of your personality soon has your lover addicted and able to forgive you anything.

Unlike the other air signs, you have a reluctance to talk about what is going on inside your head. You tend to think more than most people and have a zillion different ideas coursing through your mind at any one time. Your partner may inquire what you are looking so quizzical about, but you have a

☛ *Venus, or Aphrodite, the goddess ruler of Libra*

The Mythology of Libra

Venus was the goddess of love and also the goddess of harmony. Venus is a sign of love, marriage, and the ability to attract—not just people but all kinds of experiences. However, always being receptive to both love and hurt means that Librans need to find a partner who complements their personality in order to be happy—the scales must be balanced. Librans can be judgmental, but always with kindness and never with malice. Ruled by Venus, beauty and charm are important factors in lucky Librans.

tendency to reply, "Oh nothing, darling." The way to spice up your love life is to open up a bit more to your lover. Once you get into the habit of sharing your thoughts, your libido will heat up quicker than a furnace inside a volcano.

The Libran Man

You are attracted to strong women. You will listen to your lover's problems and do their laundry. If anything, you can be a bit of a pushover, but you are in fact the perfect husband. Sexually you may like your lover to take the lead. You have the deepest respect for your partner and would not intentionally hurt her. You like to be mothered occasionally, but you also like to look after your lover. You are great at housework. You are romantic, if a little weak. You are a considerate lover, but may suffer from premature ejaculation.

FAMOUS LIBRAN MEN
Matt Damon • Michael Douglas • Eminem • John Lennon • Sting • Oscar Wilde • Tim Robbins • Will Smith

The Libran Woman

Sensitive and charming, you are the hostess with the mostest. You will look after your lover and attend to his every need, but occasionally he may wonder what really goes on underneath your perfect exterior. Are you deep or are you an airhead? He may never know because you keep your thoughts very much to yourself. The perfect wife and partner, you always strive to find balance. You will be the yang to your partner's yin. If you get moody or depressed, it is because that is your nature. Striving to be balanced can often achieve the opposite. You are eager to be sexual and like to please. Tender foreplay is right up your alley.

FAMOUS LIBRAN WOMEN
Brigitte Bardot • Catherine Zeta Jones • Gwyneth Paltrow • Susan Sarandon • Kate Winslet

A Balancing Act

Justice is one of your best qualities. You see the world as a place where everyone is equal, and you are often attracted to people from different ethnic or social backgrounds. When you are drawn to opposites, it is as if you are exploring the other side of your scales. Although you think that differences are a great idea, when you are going out with an extrovert who likes to go to bed every night at three A.M., the hideous reality soon dawns that difference in itself is not enough to sustain a relationship. However, past experience tends not to stop you from continually being drawn to people who are totally different from you!

Remember: If you are bored with your partner sexually or emotionally, look to yourself for the answer. What could you do to liven up your sex life? You have a great imagination and an abundance of sexual fantasies tucked away in your mind, so share them with your partner. Here is a good tip. Take some aromatherapy geranium oil and mix six drops into a carrier oil, like almond. Add six drops of ylang-ylang and six drops of patchouli oil (or neroli if you don't like patchouli). Ask your partner to massage you all over with this and you will feel balanced, relaxed, and ready for some sensual action!

Love Tip • Love Tip • Love

If you are in one of your Libran depressions, you are unlikely to want to make love. It is essential for you to explain this dilemma early on in relationships, particularly if you pick a water sign (Cancer, Pisces, Scorpio) or a fire sign (Aries, Leo, Sagittarius), or your partner may think that they are to blame. This can lead to major problems later.

Famous Libran Lovers

Two of the most famous Librans are with other Librans. It's a Libran celebrity fest! Another interesting aspect of these two relationships is that in both cases, there are large age gaps.

Susan Sarandon and Tim Robbins are both Librans and have an age gap of about twelve years. They have been together since 1988. Susan is typical of her sign, because she is a strong supporter of human rights and has worked diligently for UNICEF, among other organizations. Sarandon has even been arrested for protesting.

Catherine Zeta Jones and Michael Douglas have a twenty-five-year age gap and were both born on September 25. Since they met they have rarely

been apart. Their **whirlwind romance was laced with scandal**, because Douglas was still married when the affair started. Yet **no matter how skeptical** the press was at the time, their relationship seems to have worked in that quite persistent Libran way.

Both couples appear to have found that **ideal Libran balance**.

☛ *Loving Libran couple Susan Sarandon and Tim Robbins*

Balance is everything to   you, and this includes
sexuality. Spend an evening of pure indulgence with your
partner. Eat your favorite meal, create a love nest in your
living room with sheets and lots of pillows, and read
your favorite novel out loud with some fine classical
music playing in the background. Take turns to
make love, switching the dominant role so
that you can be stimulated musically,
intellectually, emotionally, and
sexually with perfect
balance.

The PROS/The CONS

The Pros Caring and gentle, you strive to form the ideal relationship. You are a great listener and communicator, and will seek to gently heal all the pain of your lover's past. You will be a lifetime companion and friend, as well as a lover. You will accept your lover as they are and genuinely adore them. You seek balance within yourself, so you will embrace your partner's differences as your own missing pieces. Thoughtful and romantic, you will try hard to fulfill your dreams of a partner.

The Cons Many Librans suffer from mood swings and mild depression. In a relationship you can conveniently forget that you have always had these swings and blame your unhappiness on your partner! Mood swings and jealousy come from a deep sense of insecurity, as the scales are never perfectly balanced for long.

If you are really upset, you will pout about it for a long time. Often you will try to please your partner and put their needs first and then resent it. This is because you are unaware of what your own needs are, having merged into the relationship so fully.

SCORPIO

October 24 – November 22

STAR PROFILE

ELEMENT	Water
KEY WORDS	Sensual, sizzling, horny, secretive, hot, difficult
ATTRACTED TO	The unobtainable, generous, open, extroverts, confidence
RULER	Pluto

Wow, sizzling Scorpio . . . we meet at last! You Scorpios are allegedly the most sexual sign of the zodiac. You are a legend in your own time, and all other star signs must bow down to your superior knowledge in terms of sexual experience and knowledge. Or should they? One of the motivating forces for you sexually is power. You know how to get others hooked into that deeply charismatic and intense Scorpio sensuality. You know just what to say and do. With just one look from those penetrating Scorpio eyes, you can draw in the most reluctant participant.

How Do I Know I'm a Scorpio?

You ooze sex appeal and are deliciously elusive. Sex appeal seems to trickle from your very pores, and although like most of the other water signs you are quietly insecure, you would never show it. A mystery of sensuality and depth, you can be spotted at a distance of ten miles, although not by any obviousness like the brash Aries or the regal Leo. It is your very quietness that allows you to be spotted. That quietness, however, cannot disguise your charisma and charm. There is something almost sinister about the way you can captivate the whole party and yet say the least. Once met or loved, you are never forgotten.

Okay. You usually get a bad rap when others find out you are a Scorpio. Some people even make the sign of the cross and run backward at thirty miles an hour to avoid your hypnotic charms. What others need to understand is that you are not as bad as you've been billed. You are just very self-protective. Even if you're hurt, you can withstand the pain to withdraw. In fact, withdrawal is one of your greatest skills. Others stamp their feet in rage; you slip away quietly and become like the invisible man or woman. No one can get hold of you or find you if you are shielding yourself.

This, of course, drives your lovers nuts and leaves them plenty of time to calm their rage and then to worry for a longer time about whether you are alive or dead. You will inevitably come back, but will never apologize for the missing weeks (or sometimes years) during which you skipped off to recover.

So why have you gotten such bad press? In your favor, you have such a magnetic charm that you are never forgotten. A piece of you remains in all those who have loved you. People have a habit of resenting that, particularly as you are very secretive and others never know if they affected you at all.

In the initial stages of a relationship, you like to play it cool. No matter how hard your heart is beating or how good the object of your affection looks, you will not let your guard down. You will, however, give your new lover the time of their life. You instinctively recognize their sexual fantasies and can quickly turn these into reality. You pierce your lover with a secret knowing that defies logic and then you draw them into what fuels your very spirit. Even so, you remain elusive. If you commit, and you show the usual Scorpio tendencies (like jealousy and possessiveness), you manage to keep yourself one step away from your partner. This is where you manifest having all the power.

No Fear

Try not to get too caught up in the intrigue of relationships. Lighten up and trust! Your cup is three-quarters full. You are blessed with an added dimension as a lover, but don't let sex and relationships become a drug or you may lose that special magic. One of your lessons is to realize that you are safe. Fear is the enemy, not love. Once you realize that, you will be able to achieve all that you want. Most people are insecure, but you tend to think that it's just you and exert a lot of energy trying to cover it up.

You Scorpios are an extreme lot: total sex gods at peace with your lover man or woman image, or loners. This sounds harsh, but that delicious sexual magic you have can be a blessing or a curse. Be confident, know that you are irresistible, and resist the urge to drown in cynicism. You have it all within you, so bring it on!

☞ *Mars, god of war, rules Scorpio along with Pluto*

Scorpio *October 24–November 22*   133

The Mythology of Scorpio

Mars and Pluto rule Scorpio (Pluto is the god of the underworld.) The seemingly demonic rulers of Scorpio are really our own shadow—the feelings that we refuse to admit, like lust, anger, and fear. Scorpio represents rebirth through a tough initiation. By facing fear and entering the underworld, rebirth is found.

As well as having two ruling planets, Scorpios have two symbols: the scorpion (that tough creature that could survive nuclear war and loves to wait in the warm shadow of your shoes to sting you) and the eagle (that proud and magnificent creature that flies high above the underworld and has a clear view of everything). Scorpios have the ability to be either of these.

*Feisty Scorpio Katharine
Hepburn and James Stewart
in* The Philadelphia Story

Steamy, Sexy Scorpios

Many people are big fans of the Scorpio lover, and think it's
something to be tried at least once. It can be like bungee
jumping—thrilling, exciting, and never forgotten. You Scorpios
should know that certain signs just love you and seem to get along
well with you: Taureans know how to handle you, and Capricorns
aren't fazed by you either.

You are an excellent lover because sex is what you were
incarnated on this earth to learn about. This may feel like
permission to seduce the universe, but hold on: The answer to your
spiritual, sexual quest lies in what sexuality and passion bring you.
The answer is within yourself. When you feel sexual, how do you
feel and what does this reveal to you? The sexual Scorpio mystery
has so much to teach you, as well as to teach your partners.

You touch the depths of your lovers with the slightest caress of
your electrically charged fingertips. Yet in a way this makes you
uneasy; you don't know what it is you've got any more than your
partner does, but you have the "it" factor.

Avoid becoming obsessed with people, or certain thoughts, or
sexual acts. If you fall into the trap of not having a lover for years
or distrusting humans as a whole, get help quick.

The Scorpion Man

Charismatic and intense, you draw your lovers in slowly, like a fly into your web of intrigue. It is impossible to get to the bottom of you as you are very enigmatic, but that's half the fun. You have lots of dark and interesting fantasies, and are possessive and hard to pin down, all at the same time. You lie like no other and your partner will never find out. If you truly love your partner, you will honor her to the last. If you don't, you will have lovers or open options all over the place. You will take your lover to the boundaries of her sexual fantasies and it will be one hell of a ride.

FAMOUS SCORPION MEN
Prince Charles • Leonardo DiCaprio • Bill Gates

The Scorpion Woman

You are probably the sexiest woman in the universe, but your lover should beware that venomous sting: You use it to protect yourself. You can be attracted to unobtainable men and often chase men who are powerful in some way. You appear to give your partner your all, but you are hiding a part of yourself in the deep freeze of your soul. If your lover melts that, he will have you forever. He should never take you for granted, and never flirt with another in front of you or you will get even, even if it takes five years. You are hot property: There is nothing you will not do. If your lover messes with you, however, he pays the price.

FAMOUS SCORPION WOMEN
Jodie Foster • Whoopi Goldberg • Katharine Hepburn • Grace Kelly • k. d. lang • Demi Moore • Julia Roberts

Famous Scorpio Lovers

Prince Charles may not exude the typical Scorpio sensuality on the surface. However, the alleged conducting of such a long extra-marital affair is a clear indication of the Scorpio ability to have two lovers at the same time or lead a double life. Scorpios love to indulge in what's hidden. Anything really naughty turns them on.

Someone who does give off the Scorpio sexual vibe is singer k. d. lang, referred to by Madonna as a female Elvis. She is very open about her sexuality and has attracted a number of female celebrity fans that just adore her.

Portrait of sensual Canadian singer k.d. lang ☞

sex tip • sex tip • sex

You Scorpios are winners!   You love all sorts of sex, and the dirtier the better. Your partner should be brave and reveal their filthiest, most secret sexual fantasy and then offer to act it out. This will make you wild with excitement and you will take your secret to the grave. One good thing about you is that you do respect a promise. A word of caution to your partner, though: You just love to trawl the unconscious desires of your lover, digging up their most hidden fantasies. But you may not be so quick to reveal your own secret desires!

The PROS/The CONS

The Pros You Scorpios are sensual and erotic. You have a certain sexual magic about you that none of the other signs have. You enter the very soul of your lover and your touch is electric. You draw your lover into your eyes and seem to caress not only their body, but also their very spirit.

The Cons You can be cold and detached. You have the ability to withhold the truth or to tell a downright lie. You can be possessive and jealous as well as unfaithful. You are a tricky character: Your partner will never get to the bottom of you because you always keep something back for yourself.

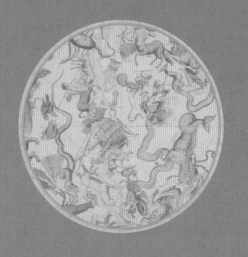

SAGITTARIUS
November 23 – December 22

STAR PROFILE

ELEMENT	Fire
KEY WORDS	Eccentric, spontaneous, unpredictable, enthusiastic, dramatic
ATTRACTED TO	Individual, extravagant, wild, open, truthful
RULER	Jupiter

Bouncy and enthusiastic, you Sagittarians charge into love with wild abandon. Love for you is an adventure, a dramatic and exciting life-or-death experience. Like all things in your world, love can also be unpredictable—for both you and your partner. The only thing that a lover of a Sagittarius is sure of is that their partner is capable of anything at any time.

The good news is that you are a stunning lover. You are as enthusiastic about sex and passion as you are about all things, and you want to explore sensuality with heated passion and extreme exuberance. Sexuality is one of your favorite forms of expression and you are damn good at it.

You are spontaneous and adventurous and can often be caught making love in the most remarkable places. A walk in the forest or a stroll in a cornfield can leave your loved one breathless with excitement, as you just love the outdoors.

Sexual Tourist

Sexual adventures and travel adventures are two of your favorite things. These two combined are your idea of paradise. You want to seek out new and uncharted territories, so a prudish mate is not for you. Whether you're swinging from the chandeliers of a European castle in a Versace outfit, having sex on a rowboat in the local park, or licking chocolate ice cream from your lover on a remote beach, your mate must take all this with the same sense of passion and drama.

Chiron, the kindly centaur, ☛
gives you plenty of love energy

The Mythology of Sagittarius

Chiron was a centaur. Unlike most centaurs, who were a bit wild and aggressive, Chiron was wise and friendly and always helpful. He was also immortal. When he was shot with a poison-tipped arrow, and was in incredible agony, the gods took pity on him and allowed him to die, rather than suffer, because of all the good deeds he had done. He was then placed in the heavens.

Sagittarians have these same traits: to love and give even when they have been wounded. You Sagittarians have the capacity to help others even when you are in emotional pain. This half-horse, half-man energy gives you tremendous verve as a lover —you can go and go!

The Sagittarian Man

Slightly less eccentric than your female compatriot, you are adventurous and excited by travel and philosophy. You have a wacky sense of humor and will have your lover in stitches showing off your circus skills. You want your partner to be exactly like you are and cannot stand pretensions. You are drawn to the kind of girl who can traipse the Amazon rain forests with you, but also look great in a dress. You will either amaze your partner with your sexual expertise, or be complete trash in the sack.

FAMOUS SAGITTARIAN MEN
Woody Allen • Jimi Hendrix •
Bruce Lee • Brad Pitt • Frank Sinatra

The SAGITTARIAN WOMAN

You are a handful; mad as a March hare, you change your mind more times than you shave your armpits. Your lover has to be quick to catch up with you as you zigzag your way through your tornado of a life. Passionate, eager, and hungry for love, you will offer it all, only to see things from a different angle the next day. You are blunt and can trample all over your lover's delicate nature, but are equally oversensitive and can take offense at the most peculiar things. You are a real goddess, though an untamed wild horse of a woman and well worth the hard work.

FAMOUS SAGITTARIAN WOMEN
Maria Callas • Nelly Furtado • Bette Midler • Sinéad O'Connor • Christina Rossetti • Anna Nicole Smith • Tina Turner

Sagittarian man Frank Sinatra with his second wife, Ava Gardner

Enthusiastic Sagittarius

Unlike Librans—who wait for just the right partner—you are willing to leap right in with any nearly suitable candidate and give it your best shot. This technique may have left your heart bruised over the years, but you certainly had fun trying. You need a lover who is perhaps slightly elusive, as well as being passionate. You cannot stand the mundane and are often seeking your fantasy partner. Perhaps, like Virgo, no one could fit all your specifications, particularly as your list changes all the time!

Actually, under that bravado, you have a pure and romantic view of love. When you do commit yourself, it is with the same oomph as the rest of your personality; all or nothing, you give 100 percent. You may have had a lover before this commitment, with whom you had fabulous passion and great fun, but there is a big difference between that and when you are committed. Commitment for you is a big deal, and you also need it in return. Misfortune will befall anyone who messes around with you in a relationship. Watch out: Plates will fly!

You love a bit of drama in and out of the bedroom and can talk for decades about all the exciting adventures you want to have with your loved one. Make sure you don't wear them out with words before you get to the bedroom, however. Let's face it: You love to make love in every room!

One of the problems you may encounter in your relationships may be because you are very impatient. You do not suffer fools gladly, and if your lover makes a mistake, you react—sometimes a little bit insensitively. You don't mean it; it's just that you just have such an abundance of energy that you're like a firecracker, reacting before thinking. Making the effort to communicate and counting to ten before you react is a great way to improve all areas with your mate. Listening is also a skill that you need to acquire, but let's stop there: You can't stand being told what to do!

Good Citizen

You have a very strong social conscience and will fight for the underdog. You expect your partner to have a similar view of life and would never date a bigot. You may have a tempestuous affair with one, but that's different! You then spend half the time arguing your point. You love to be stimulated and arguing seems to be a way that you release energy, although you may not admit this. The quest for what is right is so close to your heart that you generally have the perfect excuse!

An eternal and delightful optimist, you always see the brightest future. No matter how dire a situation seems, you always believe there is a way out. When you love, you will spill all this optimism and hope into your partner making them happy to be alive. You are pure sunshine when you feel passionate.

If your lover is not as proficient as you are, you will give them time to improve. You may hamper the progress with your blunt appraisal of their performance, but you will also see them as being capable of being the best lover in the universe. This double-edged sword approach can be said to be part of your nature. As a child of Jupiter, the planet of expansion, you believe everyone has the potential for growth.

That habit you have of putting your foot in your mouth has to be kept in check during the initial stages of passion. "Oops, that was my nipple and not the knob on a pinball machine!" Show, don't tell, should be your motto!

That bouncy, sexy, and downright charismatic approach you have to love is irresistible. You should try, however, to imagine that you are in your lover's shoes occasionally, particularly if you are accused of being changeable or moody. You leap about all over the place and are difficult to keep up with. One minute you are sappy and gentle; the next, a frenzied lover expecting instant gratification. Give your partner time to adjust and you can have it all.

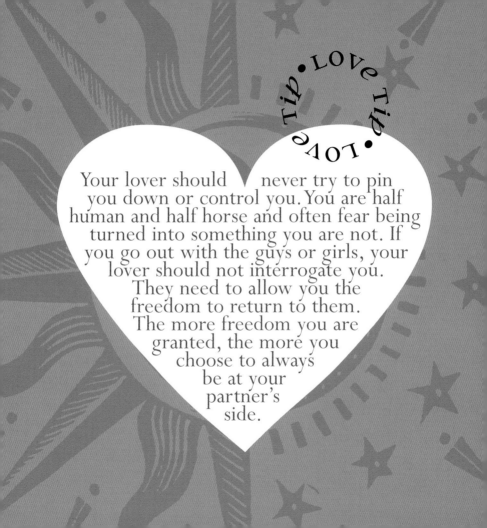

Your lover should never try to pin you down or control you. You are half human and half horse and often fear being turned into something you are not. If you go out with the guys or girls, your lover should not interrogate you. They need to allow you the freedom to return to them. The more freedom you are granted, the more you choose to always be at your partner's side.

Famous Sagittarian Lovers

Y ou can see the eccentricities of a "Saggie" lover just by looking at the famous Saggies below. Anna Nicole Smith fell in love with and married an elderly billionaire. The press went haywire and alleged that she married him for his money. We may never know the truth, but if anyone young, beautiful, and smart can fall in love with an ancient billionaire, it is definitely a Sagittarian!

Maria Callas was also a typically intense Saggie lover. She adored Aristotle Onassis and was allegedly very vocal in her expression of this. Sagittarians often have one great dramatic love that always plays on their minds even when the affair is long over.

Passionate Sagittarian opera soprano Maria Callas

sex tip • sex tip •

Your lover should plan a tryst for you, something sure to inspire you. Ask them to create an atmosphere of fun and freedom. Make a list of fantasies and adventures, such as sex on the beach or joining the milehigh club, and favorite role-playing scenes, from businessman and stripper to doctor and nurse. Also fun are day trips, perhaps to a toy store—and we're not talking about train sets! Come up with as many possibilities as you can. Write each item on glittery paper or wrapping paper and fold them into squares. Place them in a box, also covered in wrapping paper. After a romantic meal bring the box out with a pair of dice and tell your lover that they can have as many dips into the lucky box as the number you roll on the dice.

The PROS/The CONS

The Pros Enthusiastic, spontaneous, and excitedly childlike, Sagittarians just love being in love.

You will leap in with an open heart and share all of your hopes and dreams. You will reveal the magic of a natural and attentive lover. You can make love in an animalistic and intense fashion, holding nothing back and taking your partner to realms of lust that normally are only seen in the movies. When letting go, you give like no other and offer an excitement factor others can only dream of. You give your partner the ride of their life.

The Cons Your partner never quite knows where they are with you. Your changeableness is due to your human versus horse dilemma. Can you ever really give total commitment? The pull between animal and human is so strong that you are often pulled in two directions.

Eccentric and unusual, your very different view of the world is the norm. Outrageous ideas are considered your universe, and you believe that your partner is nuts if they disagree. If it's logic they are after, potential lovers should avoid you.

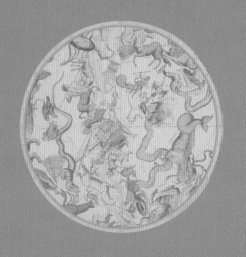

CAPRICORN
December 23 — January 20

STAR PROFILE

ELEMENT	Earth
KEY WORDS	Stubborn, tenacious, committed, hardworking, relentless
ATTRACTED TO	Softness, warmth, gentleness, emotions, kindness, honesty
RULER	Saturn

Capricorn, you are alleged to be extremely prudent in love. Indeed, you can get so caught up in mundane practicality and responsibility that you may initially fear that such lofty emotions will never consume you. Many astrologers think you are very tight-lipped about your emotions and that you only marry when you have reached a particular station in life or find a spouse who has loads of cash. They say that dollar signs turn you on, and that you are strictly ruled by convention. They also allege that you do not feel things like the rest of us and are not always capable of losing yourself in the sweet embrace of spontaneous love. In fact, they take you to be an old fuddy-duddy! You will be delighted to know that this is a load of garbage. In many ways this traditional view of Capricorns is outdated. You Cappies are intense and passionate lovers—you are not likely to shout it from the rooftops, but when you love, you love intensely. It can be said that Capricorns often have one true love in life, and if that fails (a word that sends shivers down your spine), you will never fully give yourself again.

Relax . . . You're Fabulous!

Yes, you have a practical streak and must avoid getting into a routine as a lover. If you reflect on your lovemaking technique and it has a set formula, review it immediately! If your foreplay is like painting by numbers, vary it! You have a great touch: You're an Earth sign, after all, and all Earth signs have a deep sensuality and derive rugged enjoyment from sexual union. Sex is an essential ingredient in your life, necessary to keep you fit and healthy.

When you are attracted to someone you may initially feel unworthy. Success is something that you excel at, and if you haven't yet done so, rest assured that you have a better chance than most— so get on with it. However, most Capricorns, no matter how successful they are, have periods of low self-esteem. This is probably because, unlike Pisceans, you do not believe in emotional contemplation. You think that such frivolousness is for hippies and tree huggers. You would rather build a table from a tree and put it to good use than hug it.

Unless you have some water in your chart, you think that overindulging in emotions is unnecessary and a waste of valuable time. Also, as one of the strongest star signs, you (unfortunately) tend to see emotional "weakness" as a cardinal sin.

The Mythology of Capricorn

The mythology behind Capricorn involves the god Pan. Pan had a human's body but with the legs, horns, and ears of a goat. This mixed body can represent the variations of character found within this sign—from intelligence to stupidity. The sign of the goat also has the nature of a mountain goat: Tenacious, strong-willed, and patiently enduring.

Capricorn is also said to be the Babylonian god Enki. He is often pictured as being half goat and half fish, capable of climbing the heights and swimming the depths of the world, much like any Capricorn who puts their mind to it. He is a god with great stamina and sex appeal that he shares with you, Capricorns.

Open Your Door to Love

Here is some advice: If you do let down that natural defense and open up a tiny bit to your vulnerabilities, you will get great joy. Believe it or not, you'll also get some of the security that you crave. Sharing your feelings with a partner will actually give you what you fear it will take away from you. When you reveal yourself, you will be even more alluring, and it should do you a world of good. Choose wisely, of course, as we don't want to be responsible for any hurt feelings. Especially since you Capricorns never forget anything and find it difficult to forgive.

You are hardworking and will be very handy around the house. Male or female, you have a practicality that the rest of us envy. You are quite capable of actually building a house from scratch and this kind of activity and planning goes hand in hand with your nesting instinct. If you are truly in love (or lust) with someone, you want the right environment to explore that in. Your home is very important to you and you seek refuge in your own space.

Sexually you have great stamina and the ability to go all night if the desire takes you, as long as you do not have any important responsibilities to take care of in the morning. You love to be intimate, but without too many intense emotional conversations.

You new style of Capricorns can even have more than one partner as long as you have developed a deep sense of security and confidence in yourself. This type of relationship will appeal to your independent side. Ultimately, though, your goal at some point would be to have a lover that you can respect and look up to.

sex tip • sex tip •

Your partner should be luscious, be sensual, and tease you by showing you how much they are prepared to give of themselves as a lover. They shouldn't scare you with all their wild fantasies until you feel safe—further into the relationship. They should guide you, and most important, compliment you, so you feel safe enough to give them more.

Capricorn's Perfect Partner

Your ideal mate is stable—like you—and hardworking, or so gorgeous that they can achieve success just by smiling. Yes, you Cappies can be a tad superficial (although you do secretly chastise yourself for this) and would love to date a movie star. Perhaps, however, you've learned the hard way that all that glitters is not gold. If you do get seriously involved with someone wealthy and glamorous, you may end up being their business manager or taking control of the finances. You also have to be a bit careful of trying to be controlling in a relationship or overparenting your partners. You can be very judgmental and strict, due to that strong Saturn influence. This can cause major problems in long-term relationships, as ultimately your partner may try to rebel or grow up. Often you are attracted to someone with an age difference—either older or younger.

You are generally more interested in long-term relationships in which you can build up stability and a great home life. You like to know where you stand and you also like to be the boss (even if you pretend not to be). You are turned on by other people in positions of power or wealth and admire and desire those who have achieved. Like that famous Capricorn—Elvis—you have unlimited potential, but it is not a good idea to have people around you who are "yes" people. This is particularly important in a lover. Otherwise you may well end up with a distorted view of yourself.

You have so much to offer a lover: You're great in bed when you want to be and you have unlimited staying power. Although you are said to be a bit stingy, you will only buy your partner expensive gifts, so that characterization is another unjust aspersion. If you have money, you will spend it and be generous. If you truly love someone, you will also share all that you have.

You are renowned for being very responsible and committed and so in many ways are a great catch for everyone. The only stumbling block is your need to control, which comes from that hidden but very real lack of self-worth. Others may interpret it as being selfish or self-obsessed, but it is really vulnerability in disguise. If you make your partner a prisoner or lay down too many rules, you may lose them, or at the very least break their spirit. Being a deeply honorable person, this would cause you as much harm as it does them.

The CAPRICORN MAN

You work hard, are tenacious, and love life's worldly goods. You want
your mate to dress well and to look after you. You also want her to
be traditionally feminine. You like feminine women and love to play
the strong guy. You can be dominating and have very strong opinions,
which you always assume are right. You are very good at playing the
role of father figure and like your lover to be a bit helpless.

FAMOUS CAPRICORN MEN
Muhammad Ali • David Bowie • Nicolas Cage •
Cary Grant • Martin Luther King Jr. • Elvis
Presley • J. R. R. Tolkien • Mel Gibson •
Denzel Washington

The *CAPRICORN* WOMAN

You are strong and confident and like to run the show. Although you are successful in your own field, you like a man to be a man, and have no time for wimps. You will not be told what to do unless you want to be told, but you expect your partner to take the lead without treading on your toes. Your partner must have the utmost respect for you or you will leave. You can be a tough nut to crack, but when your partner gets inside that shell, you are as sweet as caramel.

FAMOUS CAPRICORN WOMEN
Ellen DeGeneres • Ava Gardner •
Dolly Parton

Capricorn country music queen Dolly Parton

Famous Capricorn Lovers

Elvis is a prime example of a Capricorn lover who was attracted to someone quite younger than he. He may have been accused of being unfaithful, but Priscilla was his whole life. Marriage was sacred to him; no matter how apparently dysfunctional his marriage was, it's unlikely he would have left her. Rumors and mythology surround Elvis, and it is alleged that his real true love was Ann-Margret (who was pushed at the time as a female Elvis), but because he had given his commitment to Priscilla he could not change his mind. Capricorns are famous for feeling responsible for their partners.

Capricorns can often have their own agenda in

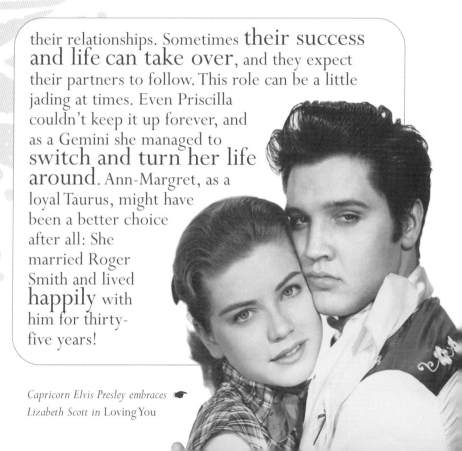

their relationships. Sometimes **their success and life can take over**, and they expect their partners to follow. This role can be a little jading at times. Even Priscilla couldn't keep it up forever, and as a Gemini she managed to **switch and turn her life around.** Ann-Margret, as a loyal Taurus, might have been a better choice after all: She married Roger Smith and lived **happily** with him for thirty-five years!

Capricorn Elvis Presley embraces ☛
Lizabeth Scott in Loving You

The PROS/The CONS

The Pros Once you commit to someone, they can relax: You aren't going anywhere. Hardworking and family oriented, you will work to make their life comfortable and secure. Security is imperative to you. You have such stamina that if your lover is a passionate person, you will fulfill all their needs. You have long-term goals and will never give up until you achieve them. With your partner you can achieve whatever you desire. You will stick with your partner even if they stop sleeping with you.

The Cons Stubborn and unreasonable, you can be very demanding and do not usually take "no" for an answer. You will persevere until you get your own way and no one could hang on longer. Foreplay is not one of your strong points, so you can be a bit basic sexually. You are also very proud and stubborn and can be resolute in your refusal to change.

Tip • LOVE Tip • LOVE

If your mate can make you smile, you will love them, so they ought to clown around and lighten you up. Express what you find challenging. Go to a roller-skating rink or do something that will please your child within. If you can enjoy the simple pleasures of life, you can open up to your mate. There is nothing that you hate more than inconsistency, so your mate should be dependable.

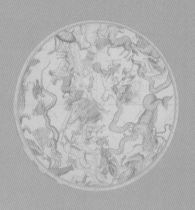

AQUARIUS
January 21 – February 19

StAR pROFile

ELEMENT	Air
KEY WORDS	Freedom, liberty, broad-minded, experimental, unconventional
ATTRACTED TO	Diversity, brilliance, spark, bizarre, honesty, unusual
RULER	Uranus

Aquarians, you are naturally excited about life and about bringing the future into the present. You demand freedom and justice for all and want society to evolve right now. You know what the future looks like and progression is natural, so where are the changes?

Your knack for "knowing" the future can sometimes obstruct your love life, because you are always one step ahead. This can be somewhat disconcerting for your partners. You may know what sort of sexual fantasy they would like to explore tomorrow; you may intuit their need for freedom or their attraction to someone else (and you are one of the few star signs to advocate non-monogamy, and are also the least jealous). However, your partner may not have gotten there yet and will think you are as batty as a fruitcake if you insist on pushing these seemingly scandalous ideas.

Not all Aquarians advocate nonmonogamy, or are as free spirited with their sexuality. Aquarians have a deep love of

humanity and when they love you, you become a personification of all of mankind! This is a heavy responsibility indeed; nonetheless, it is mutually rewarding.

You are progressive and demand and expect freedom. You cannot understand why anyone would be jealous or possessive. The whole concept of owning your sexual partner is alien to you. To you, chaining your lover would be like enslaving the world.

Dr. Freud, I Presume . . .

One of the marvelous things about you is that you love to explore the mind of your partner and, unlike Gemini, you don't ever get bored with what you unearth. The more you know someone, the more fascinated you become. This does not guarantee that you will stay with them, but it does

Ganymede, the beautiful shepherd boy ☛

The Mythology of Aquarius

Aquarius is the constellation that represents the beautiful youth Ganymede. **Ganymede was a shepherd boy** with whom Zeus fell in love, so he kidnapped Ganymede and carried him off to be the cupbearer to the gods. Zeus's **jealous sister**, Hera, was outraged. To make amends, Zeus set Ganymede's image among the stars as the constellation Aquarius, **the water carrier**. The parallel lines of the water sign are associated with electricity and magnetism.

usually guarantee that you will always like them. Like all air signs you adore knowledge, both intellectual and sexual.

You love to explore sex as if it were any other subject and you can become very explicit. The idea of sexual fantasies—and even threesomes—probably appeal to you (though if you are a conservative Aquarian, you may not like to admit this). Generally, though, outrageous sexy fantasies are probably something that you consider along with all other aspects of sensuality.

Aquarians love trying new things. If you feel you are getting bored with your partner, try doing something new with them. Sexually you need to express all different positions and types of making love. The joy about you is that you are quite happy to throw yourself in, even if you have no experience. You will enjoy role-playing: dressing up and anything that involves groups of people. You were probably the inventor of the key parties of the '60s and '70s, where all the women threw their house keys in a bowl and all the men then grabbed a key and went home with whichever wife it belonged to! Looks aren't important to you in a relationship. It is the mind and spirit of a lover that turn you on. You are quite sensitive and would not hurt your partner with infidelity. This would be talked about and out in the open.

You may attend the swingers' ball just to people-watch, but unlike shadowy Scorpio you are unlikely to participate unless it has the right atmosphere. You're adventurous, but would abhor hurting or humiliating someone in the bedroom. Sex for you is an act of exploration, an adventure that leads to enlightenment and satisfies the mind as well as the body.

All Aquarians are   individuals and thrive
in an environment where they are not judged
or controlled. You are a free spirit with
unique views and a huge heart. To get
excited, your mate must be willing to
not only experiment, but also to
be enthusiastic about the
mystery of sex and
foreplay.

Friends or Lovers?

One of the glorious things about you Aquarians is your
commitment to friendship. Indeed, you are the sign of friendship.
There is only one tricky thing for you: Are you a friend or a lover if
you sleep with someone? Aquarians are renowned for disliking
labels. This can make you mightily confused, and can doubly
confuse someone who is carrying a torch for you.

Explain that you are an elusive creature and like your freedom,
but make the boundaries clear. If you are attracted to someone and
it has potential, tell him or her. If it is just a friend that you're
feeling temporarily frisky toward, make this clear. Otherwise, you
will lose your precious friendships and potential relationships.

This is the twenty-first century, and if you want open
relationships, who are we to judge? It's your life —do what pleases
you. Clarity will help you survive this and let all your dreams come
true. There will, of course, be lovers who you want monogamy
with and perhaps even lovers toward whom you feel total
commitment. Life is a cabaret and if anyone knows this, it is you.
You cannot be labeled as faithful or unfaithful; you just travel your
own unique journey through love. Your diverse personality and love
of gentle independence is what makes you the beautiful creature

you are. Others often try to mimic you as a lover, but this is of course impossible as you are constantly changing your look, your technique, and your feelings. Aquarians are ruled by Uranus, an eccentric planet that is all about freedom. Freedom is a key word for Aquarians. You need to find a partner who finds this thrilling and can keep up with your chameleon approach.

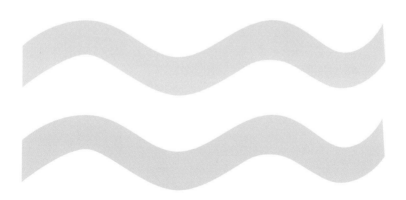

The *aquarian* man

You are very free spirited and believe that women are equal to men in all ways. You love to discuss politics and philosophy and are eager to get into your mate's brain. You may have musical tendencies and are a brilliant writer. Your mind is quicker than quicksilver and you expect your partner's to be this way, too. As a lover you are adventurous and love to explore all areas of the sexual arena. Your partner needs to be broadminded to fully appreciate you.

FAMOUS AQUARIAN MEN
Humphrey Bogart • James Dean
• Clark Gable • Bob Marley • Paul
Newman • John Travolta
• Mark Wahlberg

The *aquarian woman*

Although both male and female Aquarians have the tendency to look androgynous, this is particularly true of the Aquarian woman. You may dress boyishly or have small breasts, but you kind of like this about yourself. You want your partner to love you for your mind and to be surprised by your individuality. You must be allowed to be as free as a bird and as eccentric as you wish. Sexually you are comfortable giving and receiving, and are eager to experiment.

FAMOUS AQUARIAN WOMEN
Jennifer Aniston Pitt • Christina Ricci • Alice Walker • Oprah Winfrey

Free-spirited Aquarian Clark Gable and his wife, Carole Lombard

Sensitive Aquarius

You are a sensitive soul who would never hurt a partner deliberately but, because you feel that you need to make your intentions clear as you go along, it can sometimes turn out badly. However, your lovers love the way you can communicate about any subject. You also have a high degree of emotional intelligence. You are great at listening to others' problems and feelings.

You have a hard time pinning down your own emotions, though, and can spend hours on end analyzing your feelings. Try just feeling them and not judging them! Maybe you Aquarians are not a water sign—even though you carry a jug of it everywhere—because, like your symbol the water bearer, you tip your emotions away without realizing that these are the elixir of life! Your emotions are the secrets of a happy love life. Once you crack the code to what you feel, without letting your head get in the way, you will find sexual nirvana.

Your partner can lure you by capturing your imagination. They can woo you via e-mail and the written word. You are stimulated sexually by your mind, and the thought of doing something is practically as exciting as the reality of doing it. The more creative the situation, the better you like it. Being naughty in the back row of the movie theater, or anywhere where you may have the chance of getting caught, appeals to you. (But check the legalities of this before you continue!) Hearing a sexual fantasy whispered in your ear as you are making love should drive you into a frenzy of passion. Images and words merge in the Aquarian mind to lead to an outstanding conclusion. If your partner gets into your head sexually, you will always come back for more!

Famous Aquarian Lovers

Jennifer Aniston upset half the female population when she captured the heart of hunky Sagittarian Brad Pitt. So what is it about Ms. Aniston that made the world's sexiest man choose her? Well, both of them—if true to their star signs—are eccentric, free spirited, and individual. As an Aquarian, Jen would not have set out to trap her man but would just have been her own, inimitable self. Her love of freedom and playfulness would appeal to a wacky Sagittarian and neither desires to make demands on, or trap, the other. They are the perfect celebrity combination and it appears they have found a shelter from celebrity superficiality in each other's unique arms.

Sexy, fun Aquarian Jennifer Aniston ☛

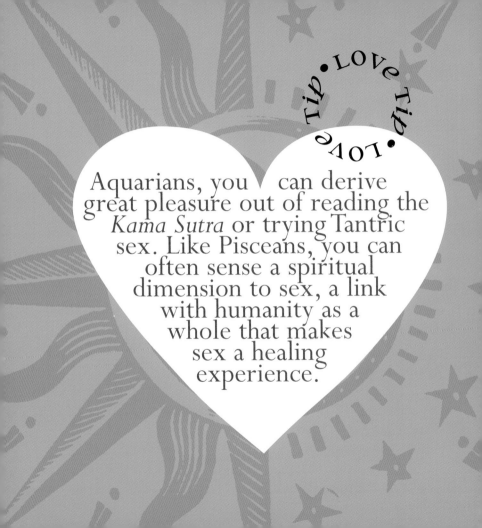

Love Tip

Aquarians, you can derive great pleasure out of reading the *Kama Sutra* or trying Tantric sex. Like Pisceans, you can often sense a spiritual dimension to sex, a link with humanity as a whole that makes sex a healing experience.

The PROS/The CONS

The Pros Exciting and free spirited, you will not tie your partner down—you will let them be free to be themselves. You have a remarkable mind and imagination. You will always be entertaining! You are also renowned for being very broad-minded and nonjudgmental, so your partner will be able to express and share all their sexual secrets and fantasies. Very creative in and out of the bedroom, you will never bore your mate.

The Cons Difficult to pin down, you do not want to be rushed into relationships or marriage. Your partner may not know the depth of your feelings and feel like they are not the most important person in your life, especially since you value friendships and freedom just as much as love. Love for you is about traveling the same road, but being free to change direction halfway.

pisces

February 20 – March 20

STAR PROFILE

ELEMENT	Water
KEY WORDS	Romantic, sensitive, gullible, dreamy, intuitive, gentle
ATTRACTED TO	Strength, creativity, warmth, integrity, romance
RULER	Neptune

Sensitive Pisces . . . if Libra is the sign of relationships and marriage, you are the sign of love itself. You know what it is to feel the heights and depths of true love and passion. Passion and sexuality are inseparable to you. A knight in shining armor or a shimmering princess is your first choice.

You still believe in fairy tales and true love, and why shouldn't you? You have probably tasted it, bitten into the fruit of love, and, okay, occasionally chomped into the odd hidden maggot here and there, but you absolutely know that your soul mate exists, or is living with you as we speak.

Fantasy and Romance

Sex, or rather making love, means so many things to you. You have an extremely romantic vision of the act of passion. You want satin sheets and candles, poetry, and a full Moon. It would also be nice if you were in a castle, snuggled up in a four-poster bed with a raging storm outside and a log fire. You may be more modern than that: It may be in a hot tub at dusk in the Arizona desert, or in a tent halfway up Mount Everest just before you reach the summit. You are the last of the great romantics.

You expect poetry and are rather good at writing it yourself. All forms of romantic expression are foreplay to you. Music also gets you in the mood, usually something soul-stirring and slow.

No one knows love like you Pisceans. The only downside is that occasionally you can live your sex life in your head, leaving no room for a flesh-and-blood lover! You have such a perfect view of love that fantasizing about it can be safer than the reality. This is particularly true if you have had a love affair that didn't work out. However, you are not just fragile and sensitive, but also psychic and intuitive. You must trust to the universe that someone even more suitable and sexy is waiting for you!

Your lover should woo you sensitively and tenderly and should be patient and not pushy. You respond to loving, romantic gestures, but also to confidence and strength. Although you love softness, you do not like wimps, so your lover has to find a balance between these two sides. Just like you, your lover needs to learn to swim in two directions to capture you in their net.

Don't let that Piscean imagination limit you: Let it carry you forward so that you can fulfill your destiny and taste true love. Being a Pisces, your thoughts and mood can literally affect your health. Since you are a magical creature, you need to be aware that to a certain extent, what you think, you create! You should therefore practice every day saying a positive affirmation such as, "I am safe and truly loved. Sensuality and peace surround me." Remember that affirmations always need to be positive, and must be set in the present.

One of your main life lessons, if you were born under the sign of the fishes, is that you are here to learn all about love and dreams. You, more than anyone, know that love and sacred sex exist. Never forget that, because belief to you is everything. Soul mate—first, sex mate—second.

Eros, the sassy little god of love ☛

The Mythology of Pisces

In Greek mythology, Aphrodite (the goddess of Love) and her son Eros were strolling by a river when they heard a destructive giant Typhon behind them. With some quick thinking, Aphrodite and Eros transformed into two fish and dove into the river, saving themselves. The likenesses of two fish were later cast into the heavens to commemorate the day that love and beauty were saved.

Eros, the third water sign, represents a dissolving of one partner into the other, including both the love and the pain.

As a water sign, when you love you are prepared to give your lover your very being, sexually, so long as they connect with your emotions. Here, you can find your perfect spiritual partner.

The Piscean Man

You are romantic and have the reputation of being a womanizer. Your partner should keep her eye on the ball, as you can be a bit flighty. You need constant romantic attention and hate domestic normality unless it involves log fires and the countryside, where you can sit, paint, and reflect. If your mate is slightly aloof and lets you woo her, you love it, as this is your favorite pastime. She should not, however, shatter your delicate ego. If she does play hard to get, you will soon be writing love notes to another.

FAMOUS PISCEAN MEN
Edgar Cayce • Albert Einstein
• Kurt Russell • Bruce Willis

The Piscean Woman

You need romance: It is the very air you breathe. You need to be held gently and whispered sweet nothings to. If your lover ignores your romantic desires, you will soon swim away to more exciting shoals. Wistful and dreamy, your head is firmly in the clouds. If your lover accepts you as you are, he will find treasure he did not know existed in your eyes.

FAMOUS PISCEAN WOMEN

Drew Barrymore • Karen Carpenter • Glenn Close • Cindy Crawford • Liza Minnelli • Anaïs Nin • Sally Jessy Raphael • Dinah Shore • Nina Simone • Sharon Stone • Elizabeth Taylor • Joanne Woodward

Romantic Piscean woman Elizabeth Taylor with her husband, Richard Burton

Beware the Dark Knight or Princess!

Occasionally Pisceans are drawn to real cads, or people who mistreat them. This masochism has to be stamped out: It is very dangerous for you, especially with your gentle spirit, to be around people who treat you badly.

Because you have two fishes swimming in different directions, you have a secret trick of turning in midstream when others least expect it. They might have thought they caught you in their net of love, and you might have given them everything and loved them with a passion. If they mistreat you, however, they may find that you are suddenly no longer available, having swum off to new mating grounds. This is often a shock to your lovers, particularly since you have made them feel like a love god or goddess! It serves them right: You are such a delicate and magical creature, a bit like a unicorn. You are here to be treasured and held gently in the arms of someone who knows your delicacy and understands your spirit and will fight to the ends of the earth to protect these.

It is almost a contradiction to be ruled by Jupiter, the planet of expansion, and Neptune, the indefinable dreamy planet (which, just like a Piscean, can be psychic, but also made up of fantasy).

The two fish of Pisces swim in different directions: Will you expand, trust, and grow or drown yourself in the Neptunian depths of total feeling? For a Pisces in love, it is essential that you find the balance between these two natures.

Sometimes you will find that you need a partner who is more down-to-earth, and it is your job to teach them the joys of romantic sex as well as the rewards they will get if they fulfill that need in you. Tantric sex comes easily to you as you are very in tune with your mystical side and value the spiritual connection that sex offers. Sex for you is not an animal act or something coarse or vulgar: It is a transcendent experience, a spiritual experience that is almost druglike for you if done with the right partner.

Pisceans are more likely to drink alcohol than any other sign. Because you are a water sign, drowning your sorrows, or indulging in too many glasses before you release yourself sexually, is a very bad idea! Drink could destroy your delicate soul and will certainly destroy your relationship. You will experience far more profound levels of excitement if you are sober. The only spirit that you should be worried about is your own.

Jealousy: the Green-Eyed Fish

One of your least appetizing traits is your ability to be very, very jealous. This comes, of course, from your deep insecurity and sensitive nature. Anyone who loves you knows that you are the perfect lover. Being jealous doesn't do you any good and can, if you start to wish for it too much, make your worst fears come true. Sometimes you are so frightened of losing your fairy-tale romance that you can turn into the big bad wolf and ruin the happy ending yourself! Talk to your partner before you jump to conclusions.

Learn to understand and believe in happy endings and trust your partner. Unless you have concrete proof, don't go looking for infidelities! Use your creative energy to dream up adventures for the bright future, which is destined to come to you.

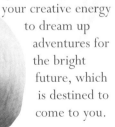

Famous Piscean Lovers

Piscean lovers seem to get it just right—like lucky Piscean Joanne Woodward, who has had a long-standing, happy marriage to Paul Newman—or totally wrong. Nina Simone and Drew Barrymore, for example, have seemingly not found the settled happiness of their Piscean compatriots.

Kurt Russell's relationship with the delicious Goldie Hawn has survived against all the Hollywood odds, perhaps due to his Piscean belief in romance. Although dogged recently by rumors of scandal, the couple are still together.

Lucky Piscean woman Joanne Woodward with husband, Paul Newman

sex tip • sex tip • sex tip

You are very responsive to love and caring. Even if your lover just picks you some daisies or makes you breakfast, you will respond to them as long as it is done with love. If your lover wants to be taken to a sexual nirvana with you, they should rent a hotel room overlooking the water, light twenty-one candles, spray the sheet with your favorite scent (this works for men and women), turn the lights low, play your favorite music in the background, and read you poetry while you watch the waves and stars. This works even better if it is poetry they have written themselves. Have some gentle toys nearby, like a peacock feather to be caressed with and perhaps some sable brushes with which your lover can paint love messages across your body in honey. They are in for a delightful surprise! A Piscean can teach their lover about other realms. Enjoy!

The PROS/The CONS

The Pros Romantic and attentive, you will take your mate to the very edge of this world and perhaps beyond with your spiritual, sensual, perfect rhythm. You can merge with your lover like no other and introduce them to gentleness, soul sex, and deep, innocent joy. Together you can be anything you desire, entering your own made-up world of love where everything is perfect and everything is accepted. This can be fairy-tale love, love just like the movies say it will be.

The Cons You sensitive Pisceans, when in fear or doubt, can be very slippery fish indeed. Sometimes it is easier to omit the truth rather than to be brutal. This can lead you to weave a fantasy not based on malice but also not based on the whole truth, leading to much confusion and heartache at a later date.

When you are really threatened you can go into paranoid mode and accuse your lover of sleeping with Mrs. or Mr. Wilson, the ninety-year-old neighbor. You will root through their stuff looking for evidence, and you can make it fit. Your lover should make you feel safe, and so they can avoid this scary part of your personality.

Dedication

For my two precious Taureans—my mother Bruna, who gave me her magic, and my son, Julien, who makes me cry with laughter and love—and also for my Pisces soul mate, who has taken me to other dimensions and shown me how powerful gentleness can be.

About the Author

Michele Knight (*www.micheleknight.com*) is a wild Aries woman who has been a psychic since birth. Her mother is a well-known Italian psychic and medium. Michele has been a media psychic for many years and regularly appears on television and is the astrologer for a magazine. Michele has been practicing intuitive astrology since the age of thirteen and lives with her Piscean soul mate, sixteen cats, and two dogs in a secluded country cottage.

Picture Credits

Pages 16–17, 22–23, 36–37, 40, 52–53, 73, 84–85, 90–91, 104, 107, 134, 148–149, 154, 168–69,184–85, 189, 200–201, 204 © Hulton Archive/Getty Images
Pages 57, 123 © Rufus F. Folkks/CORBIS, 139 © S.I.N./ CORBIS, 171 © John Springer Collection/CORBIS